D1300575

Nonviolence

Nonviolence
A Brief History

The Warsaw Lectures

John Howard Yoder

Edited by Paul Martens, Matthew Porter, and Myles Werntz

BAYLOR UNIVERSITY PRESS

© 2010 by Baylor University Press
Waco, Texas 76798

All Rights Reserved. No part of this publication may be reproduced, stored in a retrieval system, or transmitted, in any form or by any means, electronic, mechanical, photocopying, recording or otherwise, without the prior permission in writing of Baylor University Press.

Unless otherwise noted, Scripture quotations are from the New Revised Standard Version Bible, copyright 1989, Division of Christian Education of the National Council of the Churches of Christ in the United States of America. Used by permission. All rights reserved.

Front Cover Design by Cynthia Dunne, Blue Farm Graphic Design

Adolfo Pérez Esquivel, *Christ in a Poncho: Witnesses to the Nonviolent Struggles in Latin America,* trans. Robert R. Barr (Maryknoll, N.Y.: Orbis, 1983), 126–27. Copyright Orbis Books, 2010. Used by permission.

Library of Congress Cataloging-in-Publication Data

Yoder, John Howard.
  Nonviolence— a brief history : the Warsaw lectures / John Howard Yoder ; edited by Paul Martens, Matthew Porter, and Myles Werntz.
      p. cm.
  Includes index.
  ISBN 978-1-60258-256-9 (cloth : alk. paper)
  1. Nonviolence—Religious aspects—Christianity. I. Martens, Paul Henry. II. Porter, Matthew, 1969- III. Werntz, Myles. IV. Title.
  BT736.6.Y6155 2009
  261.8'73–dc22

                                        2009027673

Printed in the United States of America on acid-free paper with a minimum of 30% pcw recycled content.

Table of Contents

Foreword

Memos from Yoder

In the wake of his untimely death in December 1997, John Howard Yoder left behind numerous unpublished manuscripts, books, articles, and lectures, including the lectures he delivered on the history of nonviolence in Warsaw in May 1983, published here for the first time. But one genre of his writing is likely to remain unpublished: his memos. Yoder was a diligent and prolific author of memos. For years, he could be seen scribbling memos in barely legible handwriting on departmental stationery or yellow legal pads, in his office, in departmental meetings, and in between sessions at academic conferences. He sent them out in all directions: memos to graduate students awaiting his comments on a paper or dissertation chapter, memos to colleagues about a draft of an article or an upcoming committee meeting, memos to fellow Mennonites concerned about a son joining the military or the moral implications of paying phone tax (which originated as a war tax). Toward the end of his life, with the help of email, he was able to send out memos at an accelerated pace. And he sent them out right up to the end. One graduate student received an email memo from John that was sent forty-five minutes before he collapsed on the third floor of Decio Hall—an unceremonious way to go, but not an unlikely one for someone who spent so much of his life writing.

I was initiated into the world of Yoder's memos in the fall semester of 1996, shortly after arriving at the University of Notre Dame to teach theology. At the time, I was holding out against the newfangled, more efficient mode of communication, so it came to me the old-fashioned way: typed out on departmental stationery and placed in my mailbox. The topic of the memo was Saint Marcellus.

Marcellus, as Yoder explained in his memo, was a third-century Christian centurion in the Trajana legion who one day declared that he would no longer participate in the pagan festivals celebrated by the Roman imperial army. The incident occurred in A.D. 298 in the city of Tangiers.[1]

The story goes that one day Marcellus, "thinking about the profane goings-on at those festivals, threw down his military belt in front of the Legion, declaring in a loud voice: 'I serve Jesus Christ the everlasting King.' He then cast away the centurion's staff and arms, adding: 'With this I cease to serve your emperors, and I disdain to worship your wooden and stone gods, who are deaf and dumb idols. If such be the conditions of service that men are compelled to sacrifice to the gods and emperors, then behold, I throw away the staff and belt; I renounce the standards and refuse to serve.'" Everyone was stunned by the action. Marcellus was immediately placed in prison. At the conclusion of the festivals, he was brought before the commander of the Legion, who, upon learning of the incident, referred the case to the local governor, Aurelius Agricolanus. After hearing testimony that Marcellus "scorned the military belt, . . . declared himself to be a Christian, and in the presence of all the people . . . uttered many slanders against the gods and against Caesar," Agricolanus interrogated him. "By what madness," he asked, "were you incited so that you renounced the oaths and spoke such things?" To which Marcellus replied, "There is no madness in those who fear the Lord." Confronted with such intransigence, Agricolanus pronounced his judgment: these "acts of Marcellus . . . ought to be punished with discipline. It is my resolve to punish with death Marcellus, who served as a regular centurion, who abandoned his oath publicly, who desecrated it, and who, moreover, during the

---

[1] Here I am quoting from Albert Marrin, ed., *War and the Christian Conscience* (Chicago: Regnery, 1971), 43–45; the pertinent pages were dutifully attached to Yoder's memo.

proceedings before the governor insanely made other statements."
As he was being led away by the bailiff, Marcellus is reported to
have declared to Agricolanus, "May God bless you."

Why was Yoder bringing attention to the acts of this heroic
but obscure third-century martyr? In part, of course, it was
because Marcellus exemplified the witness of pre-Constantinian
Christianity, a topic of theological interest to Yoder throughout
his life. But in addition to this, as Yoder explained in his memo,
it was because a relic of Marcellus had found its way to the
campus of the University of Notre Dame. Referring to a page
in a book on Notre Dame by Tom Schlereth[2] (also photocopied
and attached to the memo), Yoder noted that, in keeping with
the ancient custom of venerating relics, a custom that was still
practiced by nineteenth-century French Catholics, the founder of
the University of Notre Dame, Rev. Edward Sorin, C.S.C., had
arranged to have a relic of Marcellus brought from overseas to
the wilderness of northern Indiana, whereupon he had it placed
in the base of the altar of the Basilica of the Sacred Heart. For
more than a hundred years, a relic of Marcellus had resided at
the University of Notre Dame. Yoder thought that Marcellus'
presence on campus (so to speak) should be recognized, especially
given that the fall of 1998 would mark the 1700th anniversary of
his martyrdom. Perhaps, Yoder suggested, a scholarly conference
could be held with papers on topics related to Marcellus: early
Christians in the military, the practice of venerating relics, or the
meaning of Marcellus' life and death for today. Perhaps a pamphlet could be published and distributed to pilgrims visiting the
basilica, or even a book by and for interested scholars. As it turned
out, the plan did not materialize, Yoder passed away, and the sev-
enteenth centenary of the martyrdom of Marcellus of Tangiers
came and went without ceremony, except for an early morning
Mass attended by a handful of students and faculty in the crypt
of the basilica on October 30, the day set aside on the church's
liturgical calendar for celebrating the feast of Marcellus.

---

[2] *A Spire of Faith: The University of Notre Dame's Sacred Heart Church* (South Bend,
Ind.: University of Notre Dame Alumni Association, 1991).

Still, Yoder's memo is worth remembering because it so vividly illustrates his contribution to theology and the life of the church. He pointed out aspects of Catholic belief and practice that had long been overlooked, neglected, forgotten, and entombed—like the relic of Marcellus placed in the base of the altar at the Basilica of the Sacred Heart. Yoder's primary contributions, of course, came mainly in the form of articles and books that drew attention to the largely forgotten but ever-present heart of the gospel: Jesus' teaching and example on peace and nonviolence. To our good fortune, in addition to the books by and about Yoder, many of which remain in print, we have these lectures, delivered in 1983 to the Polish Ecumenical Council and now published under the title *Nonviolence–A Brief History: The Warsaw Lectures.*

Readers familiar with Yoder's published writings will find in these lectures things old and new. Many of the central themes of *The Politics of Jesus* (published in 1972) are repeated here in distilled form. His critique of the way just war theory is used to justify virtually any war, articulated in *When War Is Unjust: Being Honest in Just-War Thinking* (1984), appears in these lectures in incipient form. And his attempt to correlate the truths of Christian practices with insights gained from sociological analysis, published in *Body Politics: Five Practices of the Christian Community Before the Watching World* (1992), is a leading emphasis in this brief volume. Still, even though these themes appear in his previously published works, it is beneficial to follow along as Yoder carefully sets aside distortions, misinterpretations, and even valid scholarly arguments that are nevertheless beside the point, in order to advance the chief and much-avoided point: to confess Jesus as Messiah entails embracing his teaching and example on nonviolence.

On the other hand, these lectures also bring forth new things. Yoder offers a generous commendation of Leo Tolstoy for identifying the "key" of the gospel: "confronting evil with suffering love," as spelled out in the Sermon on the Mount beatitudes. He also traces how this key was carried forward by Gandhi and Martin Luther King Jr., noting along the way their success in building a movement of nonviolent resistance to injustice on the basis of traditional religious beliefs and practices. And he shows that nonviolence is increasingly being embraced by Catholics, as evidenced in three "varieties of Catholic peace theology." The first is embodied in *The Catholic Worker* and the writers, activists, and movements associated with it: Thomas Merton, James Douglass, Daniel Berrigan, Pax Christi, and the Catholic Peace Fellowship. The second comes from the Catholic "professors and pastors" (John Courtney Murray, S.J.; John C. Ford, S.J.; and Popes Pius XII and John XXIII, to name a few) whose critiques of modern warfare on the basis of just war theory culminated in the U.S. Conference of Catholic Bishops' pastoral letter on war and peace, "The Challenge of Peace: God's Promise and Our Response," which was promulgated just as Yoder was delivering these lectures. The third comes out of liberation theology in Latin America, where exponents such as Dom Hélder Câmara and the artist-activist Adolfo Pérez Esquivel of Argentina were demonstrating that (in the words of the Latin American bishops in a 1977 declaration on nonviolence) "it is love, not violence or hatred, that will have the last word in history." The lesson Yoder draws from this idea serves as a blunt and abrupt conclusion to the lectures as a whole: "If that is the last word, say Câmara and Pérez Esquivel, it must be our word now."

This concluding sentence captures Yoder's eschatology in a nutshell. Christians are to live and love like Jesus, knowing, in spite of evidence to the contrary, that God's purposes will prevail with the coming of the kingdom. It is an eschatology that rejects effectiveness as the ultimate measure of moral validity, for when effectiveness becomes the ultimate measure, nonviolence is all too easily dismissed. Yoder was well aware of this pitfall, having begun his work in theology when Reinhold Niebuhr's "Christian realism" was reigning supreme. However, for Yoder, this does not mean that Christian nonviolence *cannot* or *will not* be effective, as this would imply that God's grace must be confined to the church alone and does not operate in historical movements beyond it. Yoder was aware of this pitfall as well, in two respects: in the overly narrow ecclesiology of his own peace church tradition, which he strove to correct, and in the stereotypical charge of "sectarianism" leveled by mainstream theologians, both Protestant and Catholic, who failed to see the depth and subtlety of his position. What is significant about these lectures is that Yoder avoids both pitfalls and arrives at a nuanced position that can be stated as follows: nonviolence is the norm for Christians, effective or not, but if and when this norm does prove to be effective for Christians or for any others, we should not be surprised, because Jesus is both fully human and fully divine, which means that the norm of nonviolence "works with the grain of the cosmos."

Herein lay the significance of the Tolstoy-Gandhi-King trajectory: it demonstrates the power of nonviolent thought and action working both in the church and beyond it. The same is true of the emergent varieties of Catholic peace theology: they signify the effective power of nonviolent thought and action in the church and in the world beyond it. Yoder's favorable depiction of the Catholic Worker and the "peace community" flowing from it is unusually effusive: "it is the restoration of original Christianity which we are seeing at work in our day, such as has not been the case with the same breadth and depth since the age of Francis. That is the privilege of living in our age." His account of the U.S. Conference of Catholics Bishops' pastoral letter is equally enthusiastic: the bishops are on the verge of producing "a landmark in modern Catholic thought" that "reopens the possibility of resistance as a possible Christian response to a government making unjust demands." Thus "American Catholicism has entered a new phase of civil courage and pastoral responsibility." Yoder was not temperamentally inclined to such enthusiasm. But for a man who devoted his life to arguing that Jesus is the norm in Christian ethics, and that the truth of this norm will be ultimately vindicated in history, the events in 1983 marked, for him and many others (me included), a time of profound hope that the Catholic Church was becoming (once again) a genuine peace church.

More than a quarter of a century has elapsed since these lectures were delivered. Much has happened since. Some events have borne out the hope that Yoder expressed. With the revolutions of 1989, the Communist bloc crumbled, and this, as Pope John Paul II noted in *Centesimus Annus*, "was accomplished almost everywhere by means of peaceful protest, using only the weapons of truth and justice."[3] In the summer of 1991, only months after the Persian Gulf War, La Civiltà Cattolica published an editorial approved by the Vatican that questioned the ability of modern states to wage a just war. For more than decade thereafter, the U.S. Catholic bishops, along with the Vatican, condemned the U.S.-led embargo against Iraq. And while the Bush administration prepared to launch an invasion of Iraq in 2002 and 2003, the plans were denounced in no uncertain terms by several offices of the Holy See, including the prefect of the Congregation of the Faith at the time, Joseph Cardinal Ratzinger, and the Holy Father himself, who sent an emissary to Washington, D.C. on Ash Wednesday 2003 to dissuade the administration from its reckless course. All these can be read as signs of the Catholic Church moving into a post-Constantinian posture, embracing anew the nonviolent key to the gospel. There have been, of course, countersigns to this nonviolent impulse as well: a resurgence of Catholic nationalism in the United States, recast now in terms of a "clash of civilizations" between militant Islam and the so-called Christian West; uncertainty on the part of U.S. Catholic bishops as to how to bring just war thinking to bear on the consciences of Catholics and others; and a general malaise in the mainstream churches, both Protestant and Catholic, owing to the political divisions of its members between left and right, liberal and conservative. The final outcome of history we know by faith, but its present direction remains obscure, a mysterious commingling of signs and countersigns.

We must read the signs of the times in the light of the gospel. This is what the Second Vatican Council taught us. Yoder taught us that in order to read the signs of the times rightly, we must focus on the key of the gospel, so as not to confuse Jesus' call to nonviolence with the alluring security offered by the nations and empires of this world. In this sense, these lectures come to us like a memo written years ago, pointing out things that we may

---

[3] John Paul II, Encyclical Letter Centesimus Annus (Washington, D.C.: Office for Publishing and Promotion Services, United States Catholic Conference, 1991), III.23.

be tempted to overlook or neglect or forget. They remind us that living faithfully in history comes by building peaceful, nonviolent communities in the manner of Tolstoy, Gandhi, King, Dorothy Day, and Dom Hélder Câmara: agrarian communes of prayer and retreat; houses of hospitality for service to the poor; civil disobedience against unjust laws; a discerning use of just laws on behalf of those in need; and writing in plain, direct prose about our life and work and what we believe. Many Christians trying to do these things now are doing so because of Yoder's work. His writing and teaching have had remarkable effects: his graduate students now writing and teaching their own students about the norm of Jesus; congregations reading his books for clarity and inspiration; Christian communities following his thought as a guide for practicing nonviolence in households, neighborhoods, and cities. There are clear signs of his effects near and far, in the United States and around the world.

At Notre Dame and in South Bend, his effects are especially palpable. In the years since Yoder died, many of us have continued to gather on October 30, the Feast of Saint Marcellus. At first, we gathered simply for Mass; a few years later, for a meeting of Catholics and Mennonites on peacemaking, followed by a prayer service; in recent years, for an annual celebration of "Saint Marcellus Day," including classes, speakers, and a dramatic reenactment of the martyrdom of Saint Marcellus. This past year, 500 Catholics, Mennonites, and others gathered at the Basilica of the Sacred Heart for an evening of prayer and reflection. It began with a priest addressing the assembly on the ancient practice of preserving and venerating relics. They are, he explained, material evidence of God's power in the world, signs of how our lives can be transformed into the likeness of Christ. So as it turns out, Marcellus' presence *is* being noticed, his story *is* being told, and we are encouraged to reenact his story now, in our day, in our own lives. For if it is true, as Câmara and Pérez Esquivel say, that love will have the last word in history, then it is also true, as Yoder says, that "must be our word now."

Michael J. Baxter
May 1, 2009

Introduction

Few theologians or ethicists have done as much as John Howard Yoder (1927–1997) to promote and articulate the case for Christian pacifism. As a young Mennonite, he grew up in a tradition that valued both love of neighbor and nonviolence as necessarily compatible ways of imitating Jesus. As an educated, cosmopolitan intellectual, he argued against those who sought to separate responsible love of neighbor, nonviolence, and the imitation of Jesus. The lectures collected here revisit the mutuality of these themes by arguing that nonviolence aligns with the inner logic of the created world and therefore with human social existence as God intended it. For this reason, Yoder's conclusion is that nonviolent action is, by definition, truly responsible love of the neighbor. But we are getting way ahead of ourselves.

The Setting

In May 1983, Yoder traveled to Warsaw, Poland, to deliver the series of lectures that has been reproduced here. These lectures were given amidst the confluence of pivotal events that much of the world was watching closely: the Polish Communist Party had begun to recognize its frailty; the Solidarity (*Solidarność*) Movement had discovered a newfound strength through its mass strikes in 1980 and 1981; Polish Protestants had just recently obtained access to the media in 1982; and Pope John Paul II, a native Pole who had become the leader of the Roman Catholic Church in 1979, was scheduled to visit one month after Yoder delivered these lectures.[1] Yet Yoder does not directly address any of these events in the lectures.

In a very real sense, these particular lectures were presented to an unusual audience. Yoder was invited to present these lectures by Witold Benedyktowicz, president of the Polish Ecumenical Council (PEC). Yoder's invitation was not entirely unique, as the PEC had also invited at least one other American Christian to visit Poland—none other than Billy Graham, who visited in 1978.[2] Yet Yoder makes no mention of the PEC or any of its work in these lectures. Further, what is interesting is that, in Yoder's own words, the PEC was made up of "all the non-Roman Churches, from Pentecostal to Orthodox, with Lutherans and Methodists leading in the middle."[3] Yet three of the lectures he presented were dedicated to developments in Roman Catholic theology.

To say that these lectures are misdirected, however, would be a mistake. In short, Yoder went to Warsaw to lecture on both the history and the future of nonviolence with a triad of issues in the background: (1) Should the church participate in a largely sec-

---

[1] For a much fuller account of the particular Polish dynamics during this time, see Bogdan Szajkowski, *Next to God, Poland: Politics and Religion in Contemporary Poland* (New York: St. Martin's, 1983); James E. Bjork, *Neither German nor Pole: Catholicism and National Indifference in a Central European Borderland* (Ann Arbor: University of Michigan Press, 2008); Paul Bock, "Protestantism in Czechoslovakia and Poland," in *Protestantism and Politics in Eastern Europe and Russia: The Communist and Post-Communist Eras*, ed. Sabrina Petra Ramet (Durham: Duke University Press, 1993), 93–96; and Andrej Wojtowicz, "Katholischer Sozialismus, Polen aus Protestantischer Sicht," *Evangelische Kommentare* 14, no. 7 (1981): 402–3.

[2] Witold Benedyktowicz (1921–1997) was also superintendent of the Methodist Church of Poland (1969–1983) and was also involved with the Commission for International Affairs in the World Council of Churches and the Conference of European Churches during this period. Graham's visit was at the invitation of the PEC and the Church of Christian Baptists.

[3] John Howard Yoder, "Annotated Bibliography of Unpublished Materials by JH Yoder on Nonviolence and Social Change" (unpublished paper, box 201, John Howard Yoder Collection, Mennonite Church USA Archives, Goshen, Ind., 1992).

ular social movement? (2) How should Christians approach the modes of nonviolent social protest, such as those being used by the Solidarity Movement? and (3) How should a small, minority group of non-Catholic Christians understand the current advocacy and trajectory of the Catholic Church?[4] Without addressing the Polish context directly, Yoder's Warsaw lectures indirectly address all of these issues in great detail. And it is precisely this stepping back from the limits of the Polish context that allows Yoder's lectures to continue to speak decades later.

The Shape of the Argument

Despite their apparent diversity, the eleven lectures that follow coherently trace a single trajectory: the increasing relevance of nonviolent thought and action. Yoder's argument takes four basic steps: (1) he outlines the preliminary promise of nonviolent action based on the lessons learned in the first half of the twentieth century (chapters 1–3); (2) he then moves on to counter two potentially fatal objections to the nonviolent movement (chapters 4 and 5); (3) after deflecting the objections, he returns to ground the promise of the twentieth-century movement within a rich Jewish-Christian foundation (chapters 6–8); and finally, (4) he concludes by outlining the hope for the future by illuminating how the nonviolent movement is blooming and bearing fruit within a very unlikely environment, the Roman Catholic Church (chapters 9–11).

Yoder takes the first step in his argument with three lectures that provide the impetus and operative principle for all that follows. In these first chapters, Yoder intends "to narrate in unavoidably broad strokes" the development of the heart of the

---

[4] Stefan Cardinal Wyszinski, the Polish cardinal during Solidarity, repeatedly advocated for a pluralism within the public square, i.e., the right for non-Party entities to exist and operate. But the alternatives were usually (and understandably) Catholic solutions. As Benedyktowicz would frame it, the Catholic identity of Poland was so strong that non-Catholics were occasionally viewed as being not truly Polish. See "The Place of Polish Protestantism on the Denominational Map," *News from the Polish Ecumenical Council* 19, nos. 1–2 (1987): 23.

nonviolent movement in the twentieth century. Three figures stand out in this movement, and central to this initial narration is Martin Luther King Jr., whose experiences and leadership in the American civil rights movement are documented in the second chapter. While King receives the most attention, the important contributions of Tolstoy and Gandhi prepare the way for what Yoder perceives to be the initial blossoming of the possibilities for nonviolence.

Yoder begins, in the first chapter, with Tolstoy. His purpose is not simply to use a figure more familiar to his eastern European audience. Rather, Tolstoy's work provides the "key" to both the message of Scripture and the social problems of the world: the cure for evil is suffering. Tolstoy's conversion and recognition of this key led him to reject the available establishment (violent) options and instead to choose to imagine a new path of existence. Tolstoy's key is picked up by Gandhi in a new, nonunified, non-European context, and this new context creates the social disjunction to make the next step in the nonviolent movement possible. As is well known, Gandhi lived at the intersection of two very different cultures (what Yoder refers to as Anglo-Saxon and Indian). In this context, he was able to provide a fundamentally unifying cosmological account—"an unbroken net of causation"—for how suffering might accomplish the defeat of evil. Building on Gandhi's cosmological insights, Yoder also elevates Gandhi's ability to imagine and create new forms and structures for community life that would support the nonviolent movement.

If Tolstoy is employed to provide a spiritual diagnosis, and if Gandhi is employed to provide cosmological and organizational clarity, then King is employed, as described in the second chapter, to illustrate the culmination of these complementary insights. Despite being a member of an oppressed minority, King possessed the tools and education to move between the worlds of white and black America. Drawing from both Tolstoy and Gandhi, he ultimately chose to be identified with his people, and by accepting this minority posture he was able to lead a successful campaign for justice without resorting to violence. For Yoder, King's story illustrates that there is no need to choose between suffering love and social effectiveness, and this is the argument he advances in the third chapter.

Having sketched the power and promise of the twentieth-century nonviolent experience, Yoder's second step is an equally ambitious one. His summary, in the first three chapters, suggests that the success of the nonviolent movement demands a new conception of social progress. Standing against this new conception are two major obstacles, obstacles that have traditionally presumed the "naturalness" of violence in social relations, namely, the just war tradition and sociology.

In the fourth chapter, Yoder outlines the fall and rise of the just war tradition. The thrust of his argument is that the just war tradition has never been appropriately applied, despite the fact that the concept has generally been approved by the church. In fact, Yoder argues that traditional accounts of just war have been gradually eroded by the Enlightenment and post-Enlightenment worlds. But if the principles of the just war would be applied in 1983, in the nuclear world, then the just war tradition demands the restraint and restriction of violence to the extent that it comes very close to nonviolence.[5] Because the U.S. Catholic Bishops also suggest this conclusion in their pastoral letter "The Challenge of Peace," it is not surprising that Yoder looks in their direction for support at this point.

In a rather surprising turn, the obstacles to the possibilities of nonviolence presented by empirical science are addressed in the fifth chapter. In "The Science of Conflict," Yoder attempts to deflect the challenges leveled by the prevailing presumption—in both biology and sociology—of the "truth" of the "survival of the fittest" truism. To do so, he argues that new images of social conflict have allowed the Christian doctrines of justification and reconciliation to overcome their theological isolation and engage the emerging field of conflict management. In the process, Yoder also demonstrates that Christian peacemaking must incorporate the "worldly wisdom" of psychology, sociology, and

---

[5] This argument is not much different from that offered in John Howard Yoder, *When War Is Unjust: Being Honest in Just-War Thinking* (Maryknoll, N.Y.: Orbis Books, 1984).

history whenever possible, that Christian peacemaking welcomes disciplines concerned with psychic and social wholeness as allies. Having deflected the objections, Yoder has also managed to subvert the sources of the objections—the just war tradition and the empirical sciences—to the extent that they are now cited in support of nonviolent action.

Moving to the third step in the argument, Yoder returns to focus on the religious foundation of nonviolent thought and action, the religious foundation upon which the twentieth-century lessons are grounded. Returning to ground he addresses more frequently, Yoder begins by stepping behind the alleged uniqueness of Christian nonviolence, looking back in the biblical narrative to the initial manifestations of nonviolent diaspora existence in exilic Judaism. In the sixth chapter, Yoder outlines a recovery of the Old Testament from presumptions that have elevated kingship, power, and landed existence and that have denigrated dependence on Yahweh, suffering, and exile.[6] Growing out of and following the heart of this narrative, "Jesus and Nonviolent Liberation" outlines a recovery of the gospel accounts of Jesus for the purposes of social and political ethics. Drawing upon many of the familiar themes of *The Politics of Jesus*,[7] Yoder also introduces and develops the notion of Jesus as "liberator," a theme he will return to later in the lectures when discussing Latin American Catholic peace theologies.

Following on the heels of his introduction of Jesus, Yoder again returns, in the eighth chapter, to one particular theme contained in the postresurrection biblical narrative: the "principalities" and "powers." Drawing on the work of Hendrik Berkhof, he identifies elements of early Christian cosmology that might serve as a corrective to commonly held assumptions about the cosmos, about the way in which power works.[8] The *exousiae* of apostolic witness can

---

[6] Many of the texts organized around this theme are published in John Howard Yoder, *The Jewish-Christian Schism Revisited*, ed. Michael G. Cartwright and Peter Ochs (Grand Rapids: Eerdmans, 2003).

[7] John Howard Yoder, *The Politics of Jesus: Vicit Agnus Noster* (Grand Rapids: Eerdmans, 1972).

[8] See Yoder's translation of Hendrik Berkhof's *Christ and the Powers* (Scottdale, Pa.: Herald, 1962).

help explain both the nature of oppressive social structures and the nature of a proper response. He concludes that, despite the apparent reign of evil and violent powers, early Christians held to apocalyptic hope because the Lamb had already overcome them, because the way of nonviolent suffering is more powerful than the way of violence, because this is the way the world really works.

The fourth and final step in the argument returns to the latter half of the twentieth century. Yoder uses the final three chapters to provide an extended engagement with select contemporary Roman Catholic movements in light of the previous claims, an engagement that was likely of no small importance to his initial audience. First, Yoder points to examples of Roman Catholic spirituality that demand nonviolence by drawing on the notion of the absolute law of God and the need for the cultivation of virtue. He illustrates how this spirituality is bearing fruit, especially in America, where Dorothy Day and the Catholic Worker Movement serve as the vanguard of Roman Catholic witnesses to the power and effectiveness of nonviolence. Second, Yoder describes how this initially lay movement has an academic and clerical counterpart. Specifically, he describes how Roman Catholic professors such as John A. Ryan and John Courtney Murray and bishops such as Raymond Hunthausen have displayed an increased willingness and desire to speak to the issue of nonviolence and an increased willingness to engage in dialogue and study that may stand in opposition to prevailing American political and military objectives. Finally, drawing on the work of Dom Hélder Câmara and Adolfo Pérez Esquivel, Yoder engages developments in Latin American liberation theology in order to demonstrate that, despite its contested and occasionally violent manifestations, true liberation can only be achieved through nonviolent thought and action.

Looking back, one can see that Yoder presents us with a rich argument that is both revisionist and constructive. It is revisionist in that it revises certain historical, scientific, and political interpretations of the events of the twentieth century in order to highlight the power of nonviolent action. It is constructive in that it not only looks forward from a new past to a new, promising nonviolent future, but it also outlines how this new, promising future can be achieved.

Contexts of the Argument

By the time Yoder presents these lectures in 1983, he is no lon-ger directly challenging his Mennonite mentors, he is no longer merely preoccupied with criticizing the Niebuhr brothers, and he is no longer involved solely in intra-free church discussions. By 1983, Yoder is casting a vision that is both ecumenical and cosmopolitan.

In terms of the significant markers in Yoder's life and thought, these lectures were presented in the middle of his most energetic and productive years. He was already teaching in the Department of Theology at the University of Notre Dame, and it is clear that he was directly interacting with the diverse theo-logical and historical heritage of the Roman Catholic Church.[9] Among other international ventures, he had already spent signifi-cant time in South America (1966 and 1971) and a year at the Tantur Ecumenical Institute for Advanced Theological Studies in Israel (1975–1976), and it is evident that he had been engaged with both liberation theology and Jewish-Christian relations for some time.[10] His career-defining *The Politics of Jesus* had been published over a decade earlier (1972), and it seems that the social ethic required in the imitation of Jesus found there stands

---

[9] See, for example, John Howard Yoder, "Symposium Response to 'Christianity and Democracy: A Statement of the Institute on Religion and Democracy' by Richard J. Neuhaus," *Center Journal* (Summer 1982): 83–88; and the later John Howard Yoder, "The Challenge of Peace: A Historic Peace Church Perspective," in *Peace in a Nuclear Age: The Bishop's Pastoral Letter in Perspective*, ed. Charles J. Reid Jr. (Washington, D.C.: Catholic University of America Press, 1986), 273–90.

[10] Two papers that reveal Yoder's initial developments here are John Howard Yoder, "The Disavowal of Constantine: An Alternative Perspective on Interfaith Dialogue," in *Aspects of Interfaith Dialogue*, Tantur Yearbook, 1975–1976 (Jerusalem: Tantur Ecumenical Institute for Advanced Theological Studies, 1979); and "Minority Christianity and Messianic Judaism" (unpublished paper, "Buenos Aires" file, box 201, John Howard Yoder Collection, Mennonite Church USA Archives, Goshen, Ind., 1970).

behind these lectures.[11] And his *When War Is Unjust: Being Honest in Just-War Thinking* (1984) would be published the following year (as would *The Priestly Kingdom: Social Ethics as Gospel*), so it should surprise no one that an examination of the just war tradition should work its way into these lectures.[12] For Yoder, it seems that if something was worth writing about once, it was usually worth writing about more than once.

That is not to say that there is nothing new in these lectures. Yoder's reflections on Tolstoy, Gandhi, and King are probably the most-sustained treatments of these figures in his corpus. "The Science of Conflict" also contains an argument that is rarely intimated in his corpus, yet it provides illuminating evidence of his long-standing relationship with the Joan B. Kroc Institute for International Peace Studies at the University of Notre Dame. Further, this is Yoder's most significant and comprehensive engagement with Roman Catholic social thought to date. All of these contributions are important in their own right. But, arguably, the importance of these lectures does not lie in the individual contributions of the lectures. Rather, the importance of these lectures lies in the logic of their interrelationships.

Questions from Context

For many years prior to these lectures, Yoder had been concerned with interpreting Christianity as a communal disposition, a communal minority position vis-à-vis an established political and religious authority. In 1970, Yoder presented a lecture in Buenos Aires, Argentina—"Minority Christianity and Messianic Judaism"—in which he had already linked Latin

---

[11] See Yoder's comment on the imitation of Jesus: "There is but one realm in which the concept of imitation holds . . . This is at the point of the concrete social meaning of the cross in its relation to enmity and power. Servanthood replaces dominion, forgiveness absorbs hostility. Thus—and only thus—are we bound by New Testament thought to 'be like Jesus.'" Yoder, *The Politics of Jesus*, 131.

[12] See Yoder, *When War Is Unjust*. See also John Howard Yoder, *The Priestly Kingdom: Social Ethics as Gospel* (South Bend, Ind.: University of Notre Dame Press, 1984).

American liberation theology and Judaism through their alleged shared existence as self-conscious minority groups.[13] And since at least that time, the sociological shape of Christianity began to occupy Yoder increasingly. With the Stone Lectures, presented at Princeton Theological Seminary in February 1980, Yoder significantly developed this trajectory by announcing that ecclesiology is, in fact, social ethics, introducing the role of sacraments as instruments of social process and by outlining the politics of the church body.[14] A multitude of publications emerged in the ensuing years that refracted these themes further. Amidst this increasing activity, Yoder composed and presented the Warsaw lectures.

"The Hermeneutics of Peoplehood" is one of these publications that bookends the Warsaw lectures. The article was first published in 1982, in the *Journal of Religious Ethics*, and was later edited for inclusion in *The Priestly Kingdom* in 1984. In this article, Yoder states, "Worship is the communal cultivation of an alternative construction of society and of history."[15] This bold claim raises a question not only for "The Hermeneutics of Peoplehood" but for the Warsaw lectures as well: is *all* alternative construction of society and history worship? Or, perhaps to rephrase, what content might there be to worship other than the alternative construction of society and history? Certainly, the base criteria for the alternative construction of society and history are provided in the third lecture: (a) a roughly equivalent conviction that the course of human experience is purposive,

---

[13] See footnote 10, above.

[14] These themes were introduced in three of the Stone Lectures, and these particular ideas found their way into publication later in John Howard Yoder, "Why Ecclesiology Is Social Ethics: Gospel Ethics Versus the Wider Wisdom," in *The Royal Priesthood: Essays Ecclesiological and Ecumenical*, ed. Michael G. Cartwright (Scottdale, Pa.: Herald, 1998), 103–26; "Sacraments as Social Process: Christ the Transformer of Culture," *Theology Today* 48 (1991): 33–44; and *Body Politics: Five Practices of the Christian Community Before the Watching World* (Nashville, Tenn.: Discipleship Resources, 1992).

[15] See John Howard Yoder, "The Hermeneutics of Peoplehood: A Protestant Perspective on Practical Moral Reasoning," *Journal of Religious Ethics* 10 (1982): 40–67; also published in Yoder, *The Priestly Kingdom*, 43.

(b) that human experience is borne by the dignity of the person, and (c) that redemption is offered to the oppressor and not only to the oppressed.[16] But one may be justified in asking whether this is all that is needed to sustain nonviolent action. Or one may also be justified in asking whether even these three requirements are needed to sustain nonviolent action.

Another similar question can be raised in the first lecture when Yoder outlines the organizational insights supplied by Gandhi. Parts of the list provided on pages 25–26 look very much like the type of lists that Yoder provides when interpreting the Christian sacraments as civil imperatives.[17] Does this mean that Gandhi's religious practices and Christian communal practices "mean the same thing"? Or, to read the first, second, and last lectures together, does it matter whether the procession that provokes the oppressor is led by a Gandhi, a King, or a Câmara?

One more form of this question has been asked concerning Yoder's construal of Jewish-Christian relations according to the shared nonviolent convictions held in common. Peter Ochs states, "We should be troubled, for example, by Yoder's claiming . . . that we should recognize diasporic, 'Jeremianic Judaism' as the essential thrust of first-century Judaism. . . . There is the potential here for a supersessionist strategy."[18] What worries Ochs is a monolingual interpretation of Judaism that sneaks in a nonviolent, Christian norm which requires Judaism to fit the Jeremianic definition. But what these lectures demonstrate is that Judaism is not the only thing required to align itself within this norm. Hinduism, biology, sociology, history, politics, and Protestant and Roman Catholic Christianity are also held up against this same measuring stick. For Yoder, the "real world,"[19]

---

[16] See p. 25.

[17] See, for example, the list provided in John Howard Yoder, *For the Nations* (Grand Rapids: Eerdmans, 1997), 33. Yoder further develops the sacraments as civil imperatives in Yoder, *Body Politics*.

[18] See Peter Ochs, "Commentary," in Yoder, *The Jewish-Christian Schism Revisited*, 68. See also Alain Epp Weaver, *States of Exile: Visions of Diaspora, Witness, and Return* (Scottdale, Pa.: Herald, 2008), 37.

[19] P. 23.

the "larger pattern" of reality[20] stands behind all of these, reveal-
ing itself to those who have eyes to see: "the progress of history is
carried by the common people who suffer."[21]

For this very reason, Yoder ends in hope, a hope fueled not
only by the pioneering work achieved by Tolstoy, Gandhi, and
King; a hope fueled not only by the rapprochement between
Judaism and Christianity; a hope fueled not only by the affirmation of the empirical sciences; but a hope fueled by the internal
transformations of the quintessentially antidiasporic established
form of Christianity—the Roman Catholic Church, a hope he
thought was very relevant for the Protestant minority in Poland.
On the one hand, the lens of Yoder's Warsaw lectures provides a
tremendous avenue for ecumenical engagement and social action.
On the other hand, perhaps it is not only Jews who should be
worried about whether their particular religious convictions have
been superseded by the claims of Yoder's "larger pattern" of
reality?

Conclusion

In bringing these lectures together for publication, it is our
hope that the lectures, delivered in 1983, continue to fascinate,
intrigue, trouble, and encourage us today. For those unfamiliar
with the life and thought of John Howard Yoder, these lectures
provide an easily accessible introduction to many of the themes
that dominate Yoder's other writings. The brief summary and
contextualization sketched above are intended to introduce one
to the basic contours of these themes, to a few other places in
Yoder's corpus where the themes can be found, and to just a
few of the interpretive issues that continue to exercise those who
have spent some more time with Yoder's work.[22] For those

---

[20] P. 41.

[21] P. 23. This is a theme that Yoder also uses elsewhere. See, for example, John
Howard Yoder, "To Serve Our God and to Rule the World," *Annual of the Society of
Christian Ethics* (1988): 3–14; also published in Yoder, *The Royal Priesthood*, 137.

[22] For a bibliographic list of Yoder's publications, see Mark Thiessen Nation,
A Comprehensive Bibliography of the Writings of John Howard Yoder (Goshen, Ind.:

who have already spent many years thinking with or against Yoder, we hope that these lectures provide new insight both through his sustained treatment of themes that are relatively ignored in the rest of his corpus and through his unique interweaving of the apparently disparate themes into a rich, complex, and coherent argument. But whatever the case may be, it should be clear to all readers that these lectures are about nonviolent thought and action, and for this very reason, the lectures must be about so much more. We are all indebted to Yoder for reminding us, once again, that all of our commitments—historical, scientific, political, and religious—have profound social consequences.

In conclusion, we would like to thank Martha Yoder Maust for granting permission to publish these lectures, and Glen Stassen and Mark Thiessen Nation for encouraging their publication despite the fact that some of the content here closely echoes a couple of chapters in Yoder's *The War of the Lamb*.[23] We also want to thank Dennis Stoesz and Andrea Golden at the Mennonite Church USA Historical Committee Archives in Goshen, Indiana, for their help and their tremendous willingness to assist while we visited, and Carey Newman at Baylor University Press for his unfailing interest in seeing these lectures published. Finally, we would like to thank the Dean's Office of the College of Arts and Science and the Glenn O. Hilburn Travel Fund of Baylor University for making our research trip to Goshen possible.

Mennonite Historical Society, 1997). Two good introductory texts one might want to consider first are Mark Thiessen Nation, *John Howard Yoder: Mennonite Patience, Evangelical Witness, Catholic Convictions* (Grand Rapids: Eerdmans, 2006); and Craig A. Carter, *The Politics of the Cross: The Theology and Social Ethics of John Howard Yoder* (Grand Rapids: Brazos, 2001).

[23] John Howard Yoder, *The War of the Lamb: The Ethics of Nonviolence and Peacemaking*, ed. Mark Thiessen Nation, Glen Stassen, and Matt Hamsher (Grand Rapids: Brazos, 2009).

Note on the Text

In truth, nine of these lectures were "discovered" by accident while sifting through one of the hundreds of boxes in the John Howard Yoder Collection in the Mennonite Church USA Archives in Goshen, Indiana. Of course, Mark Thiessen Nation has catalogued these lectures in his complete bibliography of Yoder, but it was the first time any of us had seen them.[1] Copies of the two lectures that were missing from the file (chapters 5 and 6) were subsequently provided by Nation, an act of generosity for which we are very grateful.

In editing these lectures, we have attempted to interject as little as possible into the text. Many of the themes present here were revisited and expanded later in Yoder's corpus, and a form of one of these lectures ("The Science of Conflict") was also presented in the Heck Lectures (presented at the United Theology Seminary, Dayton, Ohio). It is evident that these lectures—and especially the original manuscript of "From the Wars of Joshua to Jewish Pacifism"—could benefit from further editing and revising that would yield a smoother and cleaner text.[2]

---

[1] See Mark Thiessen Nation, *A Comprehensive Bibliography of the Writings of John Howard Yoder* (Goshen, Ind.: Mennonite Historical Society, 1997).

[2] Different versions of chapters 5 and 6—"The Science of Conflict" and "From the Wars of Joshua to Jewish Pacifism"—also appear in John Howard Yoder, *The War of the Lamb: The Ethics of Nonviolence and Peacemaking*, ed. Glen Stassen, Mark Thiessen Nation, and Matt Hamsher (Grand Rapids: Brazos, 2009).

That being said, our philosophy in editing was that the particular lectures presented here capture the particular shape of a particular argument at a particular time in Yoder's intellectual development. Providing his readers with this complex and occasionally unvarnished picture was our first and highest responsibility. To this end, we have reproduced the lectures in the order in which they were initially presented. Further, we have not altered the text of the lectures except for two reasons: (1) to correct or modify grammatical constructions that either violated common grammar rules and usage or seemed virtually opaque, and (2) to include footnotes in the text that provide either bibliographic information for books Yoder mentions or brief notes that supply background information concerning people Yoder mentions in the text. Therefore, to reiterate, all of the footnotes contained in the following pages are provided by the editors and not by Yoder himself.

Finally, concerning Yoder's use of biblical passages, we have also kept his version of the passage in the text and provided the translation of the New Revised Standard Version in a footnote.

Chapter 1

The Heritage of Nonviolent Thought and Action

One of the most original cultural products of our century is our awareness of the power of organized nonviolent resistance as an instrument in the struggle for justice. One characteristic of this instrument is that its operation is often informal and decentralized. By the nature of the case, it does not create institutions of great visible power. Therefore it is not easy for historians to account for nonviolent resistance as in the telling of stories of military battles and the changing of regimes. Even those who see some of the visible phenomena of nonviolent action happening are often not sufficiently aware of the history behind them to recognize that this phenomenon is not an oddity or an accident, but the product of a religious and cultural historical development.

The secular historian will be interested in such phenomena from the purely scientific perspective of their occasional efficacy and novelty. The Christian historian will see in these experiences two further interlocked dimensions.

On the level of moral theology there is a debate going on among Christians since the fourth century concerning the moral legitimacy of violence in war or revolution. The earliest Christians, as well as most Jews since the second century, rejected violence; an exposition of their reasons does not belong in this lecture. Some Christians, since the late second century in practice—and Christian theologians beginning in the fourth century—accepted the morality of violence in war (though not yet in revolution) subject to certain limitations regarding the justification of the cause, the legitimacy of authority, and the limitation of the means.

The debate between these two kinds of Christians has not ended since the fourth century. The career of the just war theory will be described in a later lecture. An important part of that debate—and an increasingly important part as the destructiveness of war increased—was the requirement that violence be a last resort, that every other possible way of serving the cause of justice must be exhausted first. If it is discovered that nonviolent means are more effective than people had thought, while at the same time that the destructiveness of the violent means increases geometrically, then the space remaining in which "just war" reasoning can apply to justify killing will decrease accordingly. This way of making the argument does not represent the conviction of nonviolent thinkers; it does express in the more utilitarian terms of the just war tradition why the development of nonviolent philosophies and instruments presents a change in the shape of the question of the morality of killing, which is not only quantitative but qualitative.

There is also a broader theological perspective, which these considerations do not set aside or exhaust—but confirm. If it makes sense to understand the God of the Bible as having made himself known with a particular set of characteristics and purposes, then the interpretation of that nature and those purposes, with regard specifically to the shape of human conflict and liberation, is an exercise in far more than only ethics. It has to do with a doxological view of history as a whole, as the continuing liberating work of YHWH of Hosts, as the subject for Christian thanksgiving, prophecy, and hope.

Yet these specific stakes that Christian theology has in our subject matter should not lead us to twist the story ideologically. The task in this lecture shall be to narrate in unavoidably very broad strokes the way that the nonviolent movement developed. Only after the story is in full view can we see the full measure of its organic unity.

What needs to be reported in the first two segments of this description is somewhat familiar. The reason that it needs to be summarized is that we are seeking, after the fact, to discern in these foundational developments those particular elements which from a recent perspective turn out to have been the most important.

Concerning the work of Tolstoy, it is especially true that I need not come from North America to eastern Europe to describe what was said in the critical writings of the father of modern literature. What is important in this description is not what he said, but how it was that he could say it in such a way as to contribute in a peculiar manner to the continuing history which included the North Atlantic nations and their colonies.

The story I am to tell is primarily a story of the modern Western world, of the culture of the North Atlantic democracies and of their overseas colonies, especially India. But it is important to recognize that the story does not begin there. By that I do not merely mean that there is a much earlier source in the life and thought, work and teaching of Jesus Christ, or of some of the church fathers and saints; I mean as well to point to the presence of Christian nonviolent radical thought first of all in the Slavic world, in the person of Leo Tolstoy (and in other forms as well, less known because less dramatically explained, like the Doukhobor communities).[1]

Tolstoy was, without doubt, the person from eastern Europe most known and read in the West in his own time. He was known first of all for the way he told stories, and in his later years for the letters and periodical articles he wrote critiquing current events. Yet in his own mind, the most original contribution of Tolstoy was his effort to disengage the central meaning of the Christian gospel from the distortions which had been imposed upon it over the centuries by misinterpretations which had made of Christianity the religion of the oppressors.

Tolstoy was first of all a convert. His *Confession*, his *What I Believe*, and his *The Kingdom of God Is Within You* are the

---

[1] The Doukhobors were a community of Christians, originating in eighteenth-century Russia, known for their rejection of both secular government and Russian Orthodox authority. Beginning in 1799, they were periodically exiled from Russia for their rejection of authority and their antiwar stance.

interpretations of a profound change of the orientation of a person's life which took place at once from within and from without and made of him a different person than he had been before.[2]

I said that the change came from within. Especially as the story is told in his confession, there was a long period of growing inner awareness of the unworthiness of the life Tolstoy was leading. We might argue that that narration is somewhat fictionalized, made more interesting or more dramatic by painting his earlier life in dark colors or by making the turnabout more sudden and radical than it was. Perhaps his contemplating suicide was not as serious or as sudden as his account makes it. Perhaps there were several small crises rather than one great one. For our purpose, that is unimportant. What is important is the sense in which what led Tolstoy to a change of life direction was intrinsically a part of the distinctive strength which he brought to life: his ability to perceive the depths of human being and relating and to describe that perception dramatically, his great gift of narration and the ability to convince the reader that inside the personages in his stories things really were that way. Thus, when Tolstoy brought this skill at analyzing and portraying to bear on a new set of life questions, there was a quality of strong conviction about his argument. There were a multitude of readers all over the Western world ready to serve as a sounding board. If he had not been the great novelist and reteller of folk tales, he might have had the same experience, but his telling it would not have been heard.

But what we must ask about first is not the hearing but the being. His power of perception and convincing description made it possible for Tolstoy, in his new conviction, to stand or to march against the stream of hostility drawn upon him by his new views. This hostility was elicited not only from the conservative forces of empire and the orthodox ecclesiastical establishment, but also from the critical perspectives of bourgeois westernization and the

---

[2] See Leo Tolstoy, A Confession (1879; London: Hesperus, 2008); What I Believe (1882; New York: Cosimo Classics, 2007); and The Kingdom of God Is Within You: Christianity Not as a Mystic Religion but as a New Theory of Life (1893; Lenox, Mass.: Hard Press, 2006).

advocates of violent revolution. Analyzing and portraying were not simple tricks or skills which were exercised at arm's length, so to speak: they were his mind or his gift. It was in doing so that he was authentic, that he was himself, and that his conviction was irreversible.

The trigger for this change came from outside Tolstoy's own mind. It was not a product of simple organic movement in which what comes later is fully explained on the basis of what was already present. Tolstoy responded to the gospel. What "the gospel" came to mean to him was illuminated by his literary and critical skills but was not the product of those skills. They rather made only more precise and demanding the claims laid on him by a message from another world.

"The gospel" does not mean some vague reference to anything or everything in the Christian message. Within the total Christian tradition—on grounds that he can explain and argue—Tolstoy chooses the Scriptures, within the Scriptures the New Testament, within them the teachings of Jesus. At the heart of the Christian faith properly understood is not dogma or ritual, but Jesus. At the heart of the meaning of Jesus is his teaching of the kingdom of God. At the heart of that teaching is the Sermon on the Mount. At the heart of the Sermon is the contrast between what had been said by them of old and what "I now say to you." At the core of these antitheses is the love of the enemy and nonresistance to evil.

Every step of that series of concentric reductions is debatable, yet every step as well can be justified on literary and substantial grounds. The result is what Tolstoy calls simply the "key" to the Scripture message: the cure for evil is suffering. This key restores the link between the work of Christ and human obedience which had been forgotten or destroyed through the centuries.

Not only is this one dramatic and scandalous teaching of Jesus internally accredited as the key to the Scriptures; it is also the key to what is wrong with the world. It is violence and the hunger for domination that characterize our society and are to blame for the other dimensions of injustice which may be described independently such as class conflict, economic exploitation,

sexual or racial exploitation, etc. The other evils in the world
are not adequately explained by virtue of an empty formula like
"original sin," nor by means of a materialistic reduction such as a
dialectic of structural changes which has not yet reached its self-
redemption. What is wrong with the world is most fundamentally
that people respond to evil with evil and thereby aggravate the
spiral of violence.

This centering process is an inclusive rather than an exclusive
narrowing. Tolstoy does not exclude any realm of real life, in contrast to the mystic path of negation or the pietistic concentration
upon feeling. He rather centers or integrates all of life into one
organizing vision. The key opens every room of our previously
compartmentalized history.

The key to the good news is that we are freed from prolong-
ing the chain of evil causes engendering evil effects by action and
reaction in kind. By refusing to extend the chain of vengeance,
we break into the world with good news. This one key opened
the door to a restructuring of the entire universe of Christian
life and thought. There developed from it a critique of economic exploitation, of military and imperial domination, and of
westernization.

The "nonresistance" which Tolstoy called for was, in his
mind, an active strategy of resistance: he worked against the tsar-
ist regime. In his support of the Doukhobors, he supported in
principle acts of civil disobedience and noncooperation. What
is of weight for the purposes of our further analysis is the rigor
with which he refused to let the existence and power of evil be
a determining factor in defining acceptable Christian behavior.
Tolstoy had the stubborn nerve to construct an entire worldview
according to which progress in world history is the work of the
persecuted, according to which pride goes before a fall and an
empire built upon coercion is a house built upon sand.

It was that courage to have a countercosmology which seems
to have impressed Mohandas Gandhi when he came across
Tolstoy's *Kingdom of God*. It was not the authority of Jesus,
nor Tolstoy's romantic attachment to the life of the peasantry,
nor even the notion of the love of the enemy all by itself that

seems to have attracted Gandhi. It was Tolstoy's readiness to hold, on the grounds of intrinsic moral obligation, to a rejection of the dominant "realistic worldview," with its self-evident acceptance of the chain of violent causes and violent effects as properly normative for the Christian.

The "conversion" in Tolstoy's story was not what the term has often come to mean in European experience: a change in the convictions of an individual on certain debatable questions, or a change in institutional adherence whereby one henceforth belongs to that organization instead of this one. What is changed is rather Tolstoy's cosmology; he has a new truth about the way the real world goes, one which is verifiable from the facts of human experience. The world is really that way: it is an arena of domination, and it is the case that its only salvation is in the law of love. Despite appearances, it is really true of the real world that the progress of history is carried by the common people who suffer, and not by the lords and generals and prelates who dominate.

We can grant a certain romanticism in the way Tolstoy identifies humility and suffering with the particular *mushik* culture[3] within which his folktale telling is at home. His bad conscience as an aristocrat led him to equate too simply the serfdom of his village neighbors with the servanthood of Christ. But that simplification does not destroy the truth of his thesis. The way to human fulfillment and advancement, even for oneself, is not found in the life direction of people who are slowly working their way upwards within the imperial bureaucracy, whether by dint of hard work or through favoritism and fraud. That is not the way to fulfillment and achievement.

As we move from Tolstoy to Gandhi, we do not find a simple account of one turning point. Gandhi does not live at the top of a relatively unified society but at the intersection of two pluralistic worlds. To open up a breach in the world of Tolstoy had required an internal criticism, provoked both by the subjective deepening of his awareness that his life was meaningless and by the objective

---

[3] See also *muzhik* or *mujik* (Russian). It is a term that refers to the Russian peasants of pre-Communist Russia.

conflict between the gospel and the imperial orthodox vision of Christendom. The same wisdom which for Tolstoy demanded that that breach be opened and that his life be reversed is laid before Mohandas Gandhi by his living between cultures, each of them incorporating the same contradictions and injustices which Tolstoy met without showing it so blatantly. Anglo-Saxon society is responsible for the imperial occupations of India and other colonies, but it is also the source of a system of legal principles and institutions which may be appealed to to undo those injustices. Hindu society is defeatist and oppressive, yet its fundamental religious vision—far less debilitated by the acids of modernity than is religion in the West—bears the seeds of its own renewal. Living at the frontier between two worlds, learning from both and using each as the fulcrum against which to move the other, Gandhi is engaged in a pilgrimage of repeated conversion all through his life story. He points to events which changed his outlook and his policies. Often these learnings were very intellectual and abstract: that is, they came from a new mental experience with a thinker or a book. His life story is full of little "conversions": once from a book on vegetarianism, once from Tolstoy's *The Kingdom of God Is Within You*, once from John Ruskin's *Unto This Last*. Of each he reports that it revolutionized his thought.[4]

Other times his learnings were absolutely concrete. They came from some failure in his program from which he learned by being relentlessly self-critical. He could thus describe his entire strategic wisdom as "experimenting with truth."[5]

One component of Gandhi's vision which moves with Tolstoy, but beyond him, is that he understands more realistically the power of truth as force. Tolstoy affirmed that the course of human history was carried by suffering but could not explain how. Gandhi's vision of the cosmos as a unity of spiritual powers, interwoven in an unbroken net of causation, made sense out of the notion that fasting or praying or sexual continence, and

[4] See John Ruskin, *Unto This Last and Other Writings* (1860; New York: Penguin Classics, 1986).

[5] This is the title of Mohandas K. Gandhi's autobiography, *An Autobiography: The Story of My Experiments with Truth* (1940; Boston: Beacon, 1993).

above all the active renunciation of violence, could exert spiritual power—"soul force"—upon the adversary one desires not to destroy but to restore to a fuller human community. Had Gandhi been more versed in New Testament theology, he might have spoken of such a power in terms of the *logos* sustaining all of creation or of the risen Lord subjecting to his sovereignty the powers of a rebellious creation. It was simpler for him to understand the efficacy of renunciation in more Indian terms. Thus the first stage of deepening in the transition from Tolstoy to Gandhi is a more transparent cosmological account of how suffering "works."

The other side of that same progress is the development of social strategies which fit the cosmology. Out of the religious holiday of *hartal* develops the work stoppage; out of purity rituals, the boycott. Going to jail for refusal to obey an unjust law places moral pressure upon the judge and thereby upon the legislator (especially in a democratic society). The illegitimate assembly, the procession or march, provokes the oppressor to unveil his illegitimacy by lashing out, and seizes the attention of the public, including the newspaper readers of London.

Gandhi has added to Tolstoy's spiritual diagnosis both philosophical clarity and organizational genius. The organizational insights arose slowly and were practiced before they were understood. They were

a. The social basis in a communal farm/school/retreat center (the *ashram*)[6]
b. The appropriation of traditional religious forms (the fast, the procession, regular daily prayers)
c. A thoroughly popular form of journalism, eschewing any complex theory (Gandhi's writing is brief, epigrammatic, repetitive)
d. The appeal to the positive values of Anglo-Saxon law, both to the citizens' rights and the independence of the courts
e. The commitment that the adversary is to be won over, yet not defeated

[6] This is a Hindu hermitage, headed by a religious leader, where one lives in an intentional spiritual community.

f. The interpretation of civil disobedience not as obstruction or coercion but as obedience to a higher power and as refusal to cooperate in one's own oppression

g. A strong sense of fair play (Gandhi refused to press his advantage to demand more than the original goals of an action, and he would not undertake an action when the authorities were under attack from another quarter)

h. Rigorous self-discipline (Gandhi would terminate a popular action if its nonviolent discipline broke down)

i. An alternative social vision (Gandhi called it the "constructive program," and he had no interest in simply replacing English oppression, capitalism, and urbanization with Indian oppression)

j. A readiness to take positions unpopular with his own people (Gandhi criticized untouchability and Hindu-Muslim enmity).

My concern here is not a study of the Indian independence movement for its own sake but for its contribution to the civil rights movement in America, which I shall proceed to in the next lecture. We see that a broad foundation has been laid for a new vision of liberating social process.

Chapter 2

The American Civil Rights Struggle

Many of my listeners have already heard the story of the American civil rights struggle. Still, it may be helpful to review the earlier backgrounds of the experience of black Americans. Soon after the colonization of the American coast by English settlers, the importation of black workers from Africa began for commercial reasons. The movement which led to the independence of the thirteen colonies from England through the revolutionary war of 1775-1783 did not include any thought on the part of the rebels about the human dignity of slaves.

Yet there had been by that time specific protest against the institution of slavery from Quakers and Mennonites in the colony of Pennsylvania. The special history of the colony founded by William Penn on the basis of his nonviolent conviction and settled initially by numerous German Pietist communities, including the Mennonites and the Brethren, would be a worthwhile history study in the history of nonviolent social concern. Yet the strength of the slaveholding culture was in the southern colonies, and each colony had its separate legal status under the English Crown, so that the witness of Quakers and Mennonites against the institution of slavery had no effect upon those states where it was becoming a dominant economic pattern.

The first widespread wave of protest against slavery began soon after national independence in the cities of the northern seaboard. Its moral base was clearly religious, although it could argue as well that slavery was not a good economic system, and could appeal to recent secular enlightenment philosophy to support its criticism. Most of the leaders of the early abolition movement were pacifist, as exemplified by William Lloyd Garrison.[1] Their arguments were based simply on the appeal to the New Testament rejection of violence and the general gospel vision of liberation, in ways very parallel to what Tolstoy would be discovering just a few decades later. Their arguments were paralleled by British counterparts, also moved by evangelical piety, who successfully got the British government to outlaw the international commerce in slaves.

Meanwhile, by contrast, the slave society was increasingly entrenched in the American South, with the moralistic criticism from outside serving only to deepen the defensiveness of the landowners and governments of the Southern states. Around 1850, the unity between the nonresistant movement and the abolition movement broke apart. The cause of outlawing slavery was increasingly transformed into a matter of regional, political, and economic conflict, which for want of any higher vision of statesmanship took the path toward war. This became the most costly military conflict of American history, ending with the formal emancipation of slaves. The military solution was, however, no solution. The imperatives of restoring domestic government in the defeated Southern states soon led to a new coalition between the federal government and white elites in the South, under the label of "reconstruction." The legal status of slavery was not restored, but very rapidly a set of laws were established protecting racial segregation in every aspect of social life. It was made almost impossible for black Americans to vote, very difficult for them to obtain education, and illegal for them to receive equal services in public places.

There were some ameliorative measures of nongovernmental character, such as schools and colleges for black young people, created in the South with the assistance of Christians from the North. There were some areas such as music, and later sports,

[1] William Lloyd Garrison (1805–1879) was an American abolitionist, best known for his role in founding the abolitionist newspaper *The Liberator* and the American Anti-Slavery Society.

where the special skills or cultural power of blacks won exceptional recognition sooner, but these embellishments were not fundamental change. A few found greater economic opportunity by moving from the southern countryside to the northern cities: but that promise was deceptive, as they soon found themselves the victims of other less legal but equally powerful forms of discrimination.

Volunteer agencies based in the North, like the National Association for the Advancement of Colored People (NAACP), struggled patiently through the use of the courts to enlarge bit by bit the realm of freedom for blacks, but progress was very slow.

One of the small victories in the use of the courts was a landmark decision by the federal Supreme Court in 1954, ruling that racially segregated schools could not be considered legal even if it were claimed that the equality of the education offered was equal. The earlier doctrine of "separate but equal" public facilities had been accepted by the courts until then. In matter of fact, the public schools operated by the southern states for the black children never were equal in terms of facilities, funds, or the education level and number of their teachers, but the "separate but equal" doctrine had protected those other forms of discrimination from criticism. This decision had the advantage of providing grounds for federal government intervention in the southern states more directly than before.

To understand the complexity of this racial combat, it should be remembered that, legally speaking, the United States does not have a centralized government like that of France or Poland but is rather a federation (somewhat like Switzerland) of partially autonomous states. Each state has its own legislature, its own laws, and its own law enforcement. Only in major critical circumstances can the federal administration override local laws, and then only through processes taking account of the checks and balances which are intended to avoid the abuse of central authority. When the federal laws reject racial segregation, federal authorities do not have immediate power to overrule state laws; they must rather be dismantled through a long process of further litigation and negotiation.

Thus, when Martin Luther King Jr. took up his responsibilities as the young pastor of Dexter Avenue Baptist Church in
Montgomery, Alabama, the time was ripe for change. Impatience
was growing, and the level of federal involvement was giving blacks
some slight ground for hope. Although fully representative of the
black Baptist culture of the American South, Martin Luther King
Jr. was also, after the model of Moses, one who had benefited
from the educational resources of the wider white society. The
white Protestant churches of the North, following the collapse
of the liberation effort after the Civil War, planted a network of
quality colleges for black students in the South. Although the
basic educational opportunities in schools supported by the state
were greatly handicapped because of the segregated public school
system, these colleges represented a strategic corrective, one of the
most creative contributions which the white Christians from the
North could make. Morehouse College was such an institution,
where King studied, like his father before him, supported by the
Baptists of the North. This education qualified him to continue
in the liberal Baptist divinity school of Crozer in Pennsylvania.[2]
It was in the second year at Crozer that he first became aware
of the achievements of Gandhi. The turning point in King's
young adult sense of mission seems to have been this discovery
of the importance of Gandhi. Before this discovery, he knew
about Christian pacifism and nonviolence, but he was not aware
either of the theological power of its rootage in the cross of Jesus
Christ nor of the social power of organized resistance. Although
he spent ten more years preparing to implement that vision in
effective social leadership, this was the foundation on which he
was to build later. His excellent academic record there catapulted
him into a successful doctoral program in the Boston University
School of Theology (Methodist).[3]

---

[2] Crozer Divinity School was a multidenominational divinity school located in
Upland, Pennsylvania. In 1970 the school merged with Colgate Rochester Divinity
School in Rochester, New York.

[3] The Boston University School of Theology grew out of the Newbury Biblical
Institute (established in 1834), becoming part of Boston University and a professional graduate school in 1871.

With that academic preparation, he could have entered divinity school or college teaching or administration, but instead he chose to return to the congregational pastorate. To this he brought an exceptional understanding of white liberal Protestant thought and of the American democratic vision as understood by the cultural leaders of the eastern seaboard.

My reference to the model of Moses did only not mean that King was equipped with cultural information and educational credentials in order to understand the white world. Perhaps more important is that, since those qualifications would have prepared him to move to the urban academic North or to a prosperous middle-class black congregational ministry in the North, his choice to return to the South and accept the pastoral leadership of the Dexter Avenue Baptist Church in Montgomery, Alabama, was a voluntary act of identification with the cause of oppressed black Americans. Unlike the majority of his fellow blacks, he was not unable to "get out" of the South. Like others within those churches, he was not still on the way "up and out" by means of professional advancement. His turning back to identify with the cause qualified him to speak for victims of racial discrimination, while his education qualified him to understand the culture he was seeking to change.

An important component of that power from the wider society was of course the official liberal democratic vision of the founding documents of the American republic. Just as Gandhi, a British subject admitted to the London Bar, could appeal to the British sense of due process and the rights of all citizens under the common law, so King could use the egalitarian American vision of the rights of citizens, the independent judiciary, and the tension between federal and state law. If our concern here were to debate the number of cultures in which this kind of nonviolent action can be effective, this use of the virtues of Anglo-Saxon society by Gandhi and King would of course point to the possibility that in some other cultures the same methods might not have the same effectiveness.

While King was faithful to Gandhi in making religion the foundation of his movement, his situation was quite distinct in the ways in which black Baptist religion is different from Hinduism. Hinduism is the ancient religion of a majority culture, pluralistic as to values and conservative as to politics. Black Baptist religion was a response to oppression, highly unified as to values, voluntary as to membership, and politically critical although dualistic. Whereas Hinduism would form an *ashram* around the personality of its guru and the special disciplines of a spiritual retreat, Baptist polity could find in every hamlet and on every city block a congregation, joining not only in worship but in extended family solidarity and moral uplift. Throughout the South, where the state, the commercial system, and the educational system were all under white domination, the churches were for blacks the arena where leadership, self-esteem, and community solidarity were cultivated without white interference, where countercultural consciousness and an alternative interpretation of social history could be maintained.

It is not only important that the church base of the movement was black but also that it was Baptist. As contrasted with other forms of Christianity, baptistic piety makes indispensable the personal, mature, and often dramatic religious decision of the individual. There is no cultic ritual which can be carried on around the altar independent of the believer's own participation. There is no self-perpetuating hierarchy which keeps the structure of the church going until some special crisis may make an individual need its ceremonial ministrations. Only personal conversion makes one a member of a community through adult baptism. The worship experience commemorates, renews, prolongs, and projects the drama of conversion into a series of renewed calls to decision and commitment. When then the bus boycott movement broke out spontaneously in Montgomery, the rallies held every evening in the churches were a simple transposition of the format of revival-preaching indigenous assemblies, which the participants were already accustomed to attending periodically, for the purpose of being newly awakened in their Christian commitment.

Although Gandhi could write and speak clearly, he was in no way rhetorically gifted; King possessed and was not ashamed to exploit the skills of the preacher, which are also a necessary part of Baptist leadership. Although King was excellently educated and informed, he did not seek to create an organization or to sensitize his own church to the possibilities of nonviolent struggle. Upon his return to Alabama, he served his community in ordinary pastoral tasks and renewed his understanding of how the South had changed since he left Morehouse College for study in the North.

The trigger which initiated a mass movement was spontaneous. At that time, it was the universal practice of transportation systems to require racial segregation on the urban buses. Mrs. Rosa Parks, tired after a day of housekeeping work, sat near the front of the bus, where there was a space free. She was not, in fact, in the seats reserved for whites. She and other black passengers had already taken their seats in the first row of the black section of the bus. When the seats reserved for whites were full, they had the customary right to preempt the places further back. Thus the driver asked four persons in the front row of the back (black) section to give up their seats for white people. Mrs. Parks refused and was expelled from the bus and arrested. The driver could have let the matter pass but chose instead to dramatize the issue by expelling her from the bus. That was Thursday evening, December 1, 1955. It gave the churches until Monday to organize their response.

An immediate brushfire of community resentment swept across the black neighborhoods of Montgomery; a spontaneous boycott action had been born. King had done nothing to provoke this event, nor could one say that he was lying in wait for it. Yet he and his colleagues knew what to do about it. The first rallies held in Baptist churches to protest the segregationist measure and coordinate the boycott were in fact convened by other leaders, not by King. Yet within a few hours he had been chosen the coordinator of the effort.

Monday, December 5, was a complete success. That evening, the Montgomery Improvement Association was created to coordinate the effort, with King elected as its president. As one biographer says, "not the most radical, not the most experienced, not the best known, he was the most recent arrival, but he made a handsome appearance and was not identified with any faction: an ideal compromise candidate."[4]

The next threshold of moral power was January 30, 1956, when a bomb was planted in front of King's home. There was fortunately no loss of life, but thousands of angry black neighbors, armed with knives, guns, and sticks, had gathered around the home by the time King himself arrived. They were prepared for a riot. Facing the crowd from the blasted porch of his home, he urged them to take their weapons home: "We cannot solve this problem through retaliatory violence . . . we must meet hate with love . . . I did not start this boycott. I was asked by you to serve as your spokesman. I want to be known the length and breadth of the land that if I am stopped, this movement will not stop. What we are doing is just, and God is with us."[5]

From that time on, King's stature as leader was unimpeachable. We have no time for a full narrative from here through the next decade. I must limit myself to a very brief list of events, named without detail. A summary narration of the pivotal events of the next decade would include

a. On November 13, 1956, the United States Supreme Court declared unconstitutional the state and local laws providing for segregated transportation facilities. The document confirming this ruling reached Montgomery December 20, and the next morning the blacks were on the buses.

b. In September 1958, King's book *Stride Toward Freedom* was published.[6]

c. In February 1959, King visited India and conversed with the heirs and interpreters of Gandhi.

---

[4] William Robert Miller, *Martin Luther King, Jr.: His Life, Martyrdom, and Meaning for the World* (New York: Weybright and Talley, 1968), 38.

[5] Cited in Taylor Branch, *Parting the Waters: America in the King Years 1954-63* (New York: Simon and Schuster, 1988), 166.

[6] Martin Luther King Jr., *Stride Toward Freedom: The Montgomery Story* (New York: Harper, 1958).

d. In January 1960, King resigned from his pastoral responsibilities in order to give full time to the leadership of the Southern Christian Leadership Conference in Atlanta.

e. On January 31, 1960, university students spontaneously initiated a sit-in in a lunch counter; by the end of March, the movement is present in at least fifty cities.

f. On October 19, 1960, King joined the sit-in movement by asking for service in a department restaurant in Atlanta. He was jailed, but John F. Kennedy, a candidate in the presidential election two weeks from then, intervened to secure his bond. The campaign for integrated services in stores and restaurants in Atlanta was to take two more years.

g. In May 1961, after segregation of transportation facilities had been ruled illegal in interstate travel, a mixed group of "freedom riders" traveled from Washington, D.C. through the South. The local white police generally refused to intervene in the riots which met the bus at major stations. Freedom rides continued for half a year, until the federal government enforced compliance with the law.

h. Nineteen sixty-three was the centennial of Abraham Lincoln's Emancipation Proclamation and provided a special occasion to remind the nation of unfulfilled promises of justice. The major campaign of this year was in the industrial city of Birmingham, and it sought an end to discrimination in the workplace and in stores and restaurants. Continuing white resistance included the bombing of a Baptist Sunday school in which four small girls were killed and twenty-three other children injured. King's greatest persuasive powers were again needed to prevent the crowds' exploding into violent retaliation. The police's use of fire hoses and dogs was observed nationwide on television and contributed powerfully to the development of public support over federal government intervention.

i. The August 28, 1963, March on Washington celebrated the centennial of "emancipation" by bringing to the capitol city the largest crowd ever gathered there; the March called not only for the right to vote but also for the right to work. King's

famous address spoke of Lincoln's proclamation as a check
which was yet to be cashed and concluded with his famous
"dream" passage.[7]

j. In the fall of 1964, King was awarded the Nobel Peace Prize.
    For the first time, he began to think of the American black
    movement as having worldwide implications, and he began to
    take account of South Africa and of Vietnam.

k. In February 1965, Selma, Alabama, was chosen as the location
    for a drive concentrating especially on the right to register to
    vote. The ensuing clash was aggravated by the intervention
    of state government, and was concluded March 15 with the
    decision of President Lyndon B. Johnson to intervene and to
    recommend a voting rights bill to Congress.

l. That same summer, King committed himself and his agency
    against the war in Vietnam. This was against the advice of
    many of his coworkers, who felt that the ability to achieve
    black rights should not be jeopardized for another cause.

From then on the movement diversified, reaching into the
Northern states (especially Chicago) with an accent on housing
segregation, and decentralized in favor of the initiative of many
local groups. The maturing of the agency naturally gave increasing
space for internal debates about tactics. The firmness of King's
commitment to nonviolence began to be disavowed by younger
critics, although no such critic ever could contest his leadership
stature, or replace him after his death. The impatience of some
of them made it harder to keep occasional local demonstrations
from erupting into violence.

King's presence in Memphis, Tennessee, where he was assassinated April 4, 1968, was in support of a labor union organizing
campaign. A few days after the death of King, there appeared in
the Catholic opinion journal *Commonweal* an article by Professor
Herbert Warren Richardson: "Martin Luther King—Unsung

---

[7] See Martin Luther King Jr.'s "I have a dream" speech, reprinted in *The New
York Post*, September 1, 1963.

Theologian."[8] Although King never articulated his theology more systematically than one does it in a sermon, Richardson discerned in King an understanding of the nature of social conflict in an age of relativism and ideology. Ideological conflict is not about particular problems, and therefore it cannot be resolved in principle: "In order to overcome this kind of evil, faith does not attack the men who do evil but the structure of evil which makes men act violently. Hence there must be an *asymmetry* between the form in which evil manifests itself and the form of our opposition to evil. We should meet violence with nonviolence."[9]

We could believe that Richardson is remembering Tolstoy when he says that "the philosophy of 'black power' assumes that there must be asymmetry between the form in which evil manifests itself and the form of our own response to it. But King saw that such a symmetrical response only perpetuates the structure of evil itself." He goes on to cite King himself: " . . . to meet hate with retaliatory hate would do nothing but intensify the distance of evil in the universe. Hate begets hate; violence begets violence; toughness begets a greater toughness. We must meet the forces of hate with the power of love; we must meet physical force with soul force. Our aim must never be to defeat or humiliate the white man, but to win his friendship and understanding."[10]

Richardson continues, "King does not argue for nonviolence on a fideistic confessional ground—as if . . . a witness to the Lordship of Christ, a witness that must come in our time must always be defeated. King argues that nonviolence is the sole practical way to struggle against evil because it alone is based on a right understanding of reality itself."

In sum, in language quite his own, King has reformulated what he inherited from Gandhi, and Gandhi from Tolstoy.

---

[8] Herbert Warner Richardson, "Martin Luther King—Unsung Theologian," *Commonweal* (May 3, 1968): 201–3.

[9] Richardson, "Martin Luther King," 202.

[10] Richardson, "Martin Luther King," 202, citing King, *Stride Toward Freedom*, 87.

There is not a disjunction between, on the one hand, taking the way of the cross as a matter of blind faith, come what may, and on the other hand rational responsibility for historical process which always needs to include violence. That disjunctive analysis itself represents a religious bias which is all the more challenge-able for its being unavowed. For those who confess the Lamb that was slain as risen Lord worthy to receive power, there can be no ultimate need to choose between suffering love and social effectiveness.

Chapter 3

The Lessons of the Nonviolent Experience

Toward the end of the Epistle to the Hebrews (chapter 11), after the author had given an extended description of the acts of faithfulness of Abel and Abraham, and a more-brief but still-concrete description of other well-known heroes, the description spreads out or splashes into a list of many other people too numerous to name. In a similar way, in the wake of the major personalities whom we have taken as prototypical (but also to some extent independently of them), there would be others to name if our purpose were doxological like that of the author of Hebrews. There are others whose creativity we would need to describe and whose sacrifices we would chronicle if our purpose were to lift from these stories a series of lessons or generalizations, as the social scientist does. Without providing those details, let it be said that those stories do exist and that their analysis would richly reinforce the lessons described above. The experiences described above are not models to be slavishly imitated. Neither, however, are they rare and odd exceptions (what in current English we call "flukes"); they are prototypes, or (to use a biblical expression) "first fruits." This is corroborated by the later "cloud of witnesses."

To that cloud of witnesses we could add the thousands of American young men who refused their call to military service in the Vietnam War and the wider circle of their friends and sympathizers who gathered in streets and lecture halls to support them. We could add the work of César Chávez, the Mexican American activist, who enabled farm laborers for the first time to grasp the right to organization and collective bargaining.[1] We could add Lanza del Vasto or Shantidas, the noble disciple of Gandhi, who brought to the West the *ashram* pattern of devotion, training, and direct action.[2] We could add Danilo Dolci, the Italian poet and architect who first imparted to the victims of Sicily's feudal or bandit culture the courage and organizational vision to defend themselves and prod even the Roman bureaucracy into action.[3] We could watch the work of Archbishop Hélder Câmara, conscience of the collegiums of the Roman Catholic bishops of Latin America in their growing courageous readiness to denounce the terrorism of states and counterstates.[4] If the information could flow freely, we could find and congratulate and analyze many others, from other portions of the world, mobilizing other victim people against other kinds of oppression. It is the global message of that common story which we need now to summarize.

The significant generalizations to lift out of these stories take us beyond questions of personality to the extent that is possible. Any powerful human figure is unique, and these men are no exception to that rule. When measured by ordinary Western standards of mental balance or intellectual consistency, both Tolstoy and Gandhi seem strange to many. Certainly, if we were to write a critical biography, we would need to take account of both person-

---

[1] César Chávez (1927–1993) was a Mexican American farmworker and civil rights activist who cofounded the National Farm Workers Association, which became the United Farm Workers of America. He is best known for his work on behalf of union laborers, using broad-based strikes and marches in the pursuit of better labor conditions.

[2] Lanza del Vasto (1901–1981), born Giuseppe Giovanni Luigi Enrico Lanza di Trabia, was an Italian philosopher and activist. A disciple of Gandhi, del Vasto founded The Community of the Ark in France in 1948 as a spiritual commune dedicated to spirituality and nonviolence.

[3] Danilo Dolci (1924–1997) is considered one of the founders of the nonviolence movement in Italy. He is best known for his writing against the Sicilian mafia and his advocacy on behalf of the poor in Sicily. He was nominated for the Nobel Peace Prize twice.

[4] Dom Hélder Câmara (1909–1999) was the Catholic archbishop of Olinda and Recife (Brazil). Câmara received the Pacem in Terris Award (1975) for his work on behalf of the Brazilian poor.

ality weaknesses which are irrelevant to social theory and some procedural weaknesses which may have something to do with the theory, such as the way in which Gandhi administered his *ashram* or Tolstoy his estate. Our purpose here is neither to pursue the beatification of these men nor to debunk them, but rather to seek to perceive through and beneath them the larger pattern which they brought to light. Our task is not biography but distillation.

Since the pragmatic cultures of western Europe and North America tend to translate everything into terms of procedure and effectiveness, it is indispensable to remember that for both Gandhi and King there is no such thing as a "technique" or "tactic" of nonviolent action which could be lifted out of its original framework of spiritual and moral community discipline and "applied" as a tactic for its own sake. A true perception of Gandhi was delayed in the West for a generation, due partly to the fact that this link between nonviolence and its original framework was not perceived. One early book interpreting Gandhi to England and America bore the title *War without Violence*,[5] as if one could proceed, as in an ordinary war, to define one's selfish goals and designate the enemy to be destroyed, and then simply choose nonviolent rather than violent weapons for the combat.

Nonviolent militancy demands a religious community discipline so that action will be common and consistent. There is not the wealth or the leisure which would permit a nonviolent community to maintain a centralized chain of command whereby orders are received from a central "general." The decisions that in a military campaign are called tactical must in a nonviolent action be decided on the basis of prior decisions of principle. This calls for a high degree of common understandings, regularly rehearsed and renewed, about the mentality of the *satyagrahi*.[6] Only a value system which is repeatedly deepened through a

---

[5] See Krishnalal Shridharani, *War without Violence: A Study of Gandhi's Methods and Its Accomplishments* (New York: Harcourt, Brace, 1939).

[6] *Satyagrahi* were developed by Gandhi as the rules of nonviolence or the disciplines necessary for the practice of *satyagraha* (active nonviolent resistance). These rules or guidelines are laid out by Gandhi in numerous places, including "Prerequisites for Satyagraha," *Young India*, August 1, 1925.

common understanding of love toward the adversary, through rehearsal of reasons why violent action is inappropriate, and through the memories of successful nonviolent actions can make it possible to count on a demonstration of noncooperation or civil disobedience to remain coherent and achieve its goals.

Nonviolent action is costly. It includes readiness at least for prison and a degree of risk of loss of life. In some of the experience of the Gandhian movement, the loss of life was as likely a prospect as it is in a strictly military encounter. Yet the willingness of people to run those risks cannot be rooted in the excitement of adventure or in chauvinistic hatred or the thrill of the risk of a duel, as it is in the military case. Where, then, can it be rooted? It can only be rooted in a religious vision of the congruence between suffering and the purposes of God.

It is not indispensible that their vision of God must be exactly that of Jews or of Christians for such a vision to guide people. Yet it does seem that, for the "faith" of the community active in nonviolence to both sustain and guide the community, there must at least be some roughly equivalent conviction that the course of human experience is purposive, that it is borne by the affirmation and not the sacrifice of the dignity of the person, and that redemption is offered to the oppressor and not only to the oppressed. Without those constitutive elements, it will not be possible to keep the defense of the rights of victims from seeking a mere reversal of roles and replacing one oppression with another.

Rooting nonviolence in a religious vision of history forbids that the renunciation of violence be thought of as a mere tactic or technique. That does not exclude the possibility that in given conflict situations there may well be participants who see it only on that level. It was the case in the civil rights struggle in the United States that the leadership of King and his Christian colleagues was accepted by some who did not consider themselves Christian; for others, the renunciation of violence was for the time being a merely "tactical move," which deprived the racist authorities of the pretext for violent retaliation. It was not wrong for either them or King to enter into a tactical alliance in particular situations. Yet it became clear, when the movement came on harder times and their tactical reasons for renouncing violence were no longer promising, that the ways needed to part. It is striking that those in America who from that point forward said that violence would be justified never did actually achieve anything positive by means of violent struggle.

The unity of religious rootage and ethical strategy is not merely intellectual. The planning meetings of the American black struggle were at the same time services of praise and preaching. The marches for freedom were at the same time religious processions, a pattern which was to be established again in another context when Bishop Hélder Câmara of Brazil used the format of the religious procession to gather people in political protest, when their manifestation would not have been otherwise legal.

Thus, before it is a social strategy, nonviolence is a moral commitment; before it is a moral commitment, it is a distinctive spirituality. It presupposes and fosters a distinctive way of seeing oneself and one's neighbor under God. That "way of seeing things" is more like prayer than it is like shrewd social strategy, although it is both. It is more a faith than it is a theory, although it is both.

Thus, what I first described as the stance of the convert is not centered upon either the suddenness or the emotional power with which an individual changed orientation, nor upon the particular doctrinal or ritual component of the new commitment. It centered rather on the newness of the world vision into which one has been brought. What is universally present and logically necessary is the presence of the following two factors:

a. The nonviolent liberator is, like Moses, at home in both worlds: that of the victims with whom he identifies freely and that of the oppressive structures which he challenges. If he were not at home in the culture he challenges, he would lack both the capacity to analyze accurately and the capacity to love his adversaries. If his adhesion to the victim community were not voluntary, his own suffering would drive him away.

b. The quality of voluntary (uncoerced) and tested commitment to a loyalty different from the one which dominates his
world sustains an alternative consciousness, a different way
not only of setting goals for the world but even of describing the facts, the way the world really is. Marxism, other
kinds of Hegelianism, and other modern and post-Fascist[7]
modern philosophies have ways of correcting for the skewing
of consciousness which is produced by the comforts and the
discomforts of the unfair world in which we have grown up.
There may be truth in several of these approaches, but not
a truth as fundamental as that to which the "convert" has
come, who has authentically chosen to leave one life behind
and to enter a different story, a different world. He is able
to bring forth the character and the power of the entire society. Conversion is therefore not a matter of emotion or of
individualism; it is the fulcrum whereby an alternative social
project gains hold on events. It is the hinge between one story
and another, between the acceptance of subjugation and the
beginning of empowerment.

For the most convinced agents of nonviolent resistance, part of
their motivation is a religious vision, but this does not mean that
secular social science analysis could not interpret what is going
on in purely secular categories. The statements that one (a) is
committed to the reconciliation of the oppressor and not only
the liberation of the oppressed; (b) that the renunciation of violence means a new relationship between adversaries; or (c) that
ends and means are inseparable, are perfectly capable of transposition into concepts quite independent of the original Christian
or Hindu theology from which they were derived. Social scientists have begun to describe the ways in which a conflict situation
is transformed by the readiness of one party to suffer, or by the
promise of one party to respect the dignity of the other, or by

[7] The original text at this point read "post-fashion philosophies." Given the
context of the sentence, the editors decided upon "post-Fascist" as what was most
likely meant by this phrase.

the commitment to truthfulness. A statement like that of Gandhi, "If they kill me, then they will have my body, but they will not have my obedience,"[8] demands a profound motivation. Yet once the statement is made, it becomes an operative component of the social process, just like anyone else's statement of what they want to have happen and what they are willing to pay for it. Gandhi and King in this way differ from Tolstoy. They incorporate and lay claim to social science analysis and social process wisdom, rather than projecting a gospel imperative as pure revealed paradox without rationality.

Logicians tell us that there are two ordinary ways to reason about morality. One can concentrate on results or ends and call good those deeds which produce good ends. Since there are many different values at stake in any complex social context, this will mean weighing many goods and evils against each other in a calculation of total utility. The other way to reason is to consider certain deeds as intrinsically virtuous or forbidden and not to be responsible for calculating the ends.

There are efforts to bridge over this polarity with mixed answers, or to bypass it with resort to some other consideration like individual virtue or community identity. Those approaches may be valid complements in their own right, but generally they do not address the question; we still need to ask how the virtuous person will decide, or what the discerning community will prefer.

The violence of the crusade and the violence of fascism represent a morality of intrinsic means: one does what is commanded because it is commanded, and not because of the assured results. The justifications of violence with a view to social goals on the other hand, according to the traditions of the just war and the just revolution, are arguments based on the pragmatism of necessary but lesser evils. The destruction of persons, relationships,

---

[8] The original quote by Gandhi—as cited in M. K. Gandhi, *The Collected Works of Mahatma Gandhi* (New Delhi: Publications Division, Ministry of Information and Broadcasting, Government of India, 1979), 162—is "They may torture my body, break my bones, even kill me, then they will have my dead body, not my obedience."

and property is recognized to be an evil, but an evil—it is held—that is our duty under the present circumstances to inflict on others for the sake of some greater good. Thus the utility/principle debate is pertinent to our topic.

None of our three men were philosophers. Each was, in his own way, quite foreign to the vigor which we normally associate with philosophical analysis. Nonetheless, each sought in his own way to make a point which ought to be given (and could be given) greater philosophical sophistication in the face of the dilemma with which we began. Each said in different ways that the means and the end cannot be separated. The means is the end in process of becoming. When, in the service of even the most valuable cause, one chooses to resort to violence, that disregard for the dignity of the neighbor and that disrespect for the social fabric have planted the seeds for the failure of one's own enterprise. Only fidelity to love as means can be an instrument for love as end.

What I have just stated can be demonstrated in terms of social science. The sociologist, the psychologist, or the historian could spell out how it has been true in social experience. There are exceptions, but on the average and in the long run they do not disprove the rule.

There is no such thing as one nonviolent strategy to be used for liberation anywhere and everywhere. The essence of nonviolent action includes charismatic creativity. It needs prophetic insight into timing and symbolism, which is more like the artist than the strategist. It demands precise analysis of social systems that is more like the sociologist than the ideologue. Nonetheless, it is possible to say that in the labors of King we have seen the maturity or the roundedness of an understanding of nonviolent liberation which could illuminate and give direction to searches in other cultures for ways to work in favor of other causes. It remains to summarize those learnings:

a. There is no enemy to be destroyed; there is an adversary to be reconciled.
b. The renunciation of violence is not a puristic legalism but a commitment to work with the grain of the cosmos, a refusal

to let the adversary declare himself outside the circle of reconciliation.

c. Unlike rifles, Molotov cocktails, or atomic bombs, nonviolence is a weapon which can only be used effectively for a good cause. Its usage consists in an appeal to the moral insight of the adversary and a transformation of a common political will. If the cause is not worthy, not only in the mind of the nonviolent demonstrator but in that of the public at large, the "weapon" will not work. Nonviolent means of struggle may be used unwisely and ineffectively and may fail; when they do fail, the damage is far less.

d. The renunciation of violence does have tactical advantages: it robs the oppressor of the pretext to aggravate his own violence, and it draws the attention of others to the justice of one's cause. But these tactical advantages are not its justification. Those who consider the justification to be on that level will not stay the course and will thereby convince themselves that it will not work.

e. The firm renunciation of violence produces a context for creativity, whereas holding open the notion of violence as last resort removes that incentive. He who claims the right to determine on his own when he is in that situation of last resort where violence is justified is thereby always on the razor's edge between two contradictory moral systems and can never fruitfully proceed with either. As César Chávez said, "If you have a gun and they do too, then you can be frightened because it becomes a question of who gets shot first. But if you have no gun . . . well, then the guy with the gun has a lot harder decision to make than you have."[9]

f. As contrasted with quietism, which sees moral purity and withdrawal, and with legalism, which conceives of conformity to law as independent of the commitment to the welfare of persons, nonviolent action assumes that the world is racked by conflict and yet willingly enters and orchestrates that conflict.

---

[9] Quoted in Marjorie Hope and James Young, *The Struggle for Humanity: Agents of Nonviolent Change in a Violent World* (Maryknoll, N.Y.: Orbis Books, 1977), 155.

Conflict is not to be avoided but to be managed in ways which safeguard the adversaries' honor. It is in that sense an extension of the instructions of Jesus telling his disciples that the response to sin is to confront the guilty person in a dialogical summons to reconciliation (Matt 18:15). The meaning of the cross: what God does with human sinfulness; the way of the cross: the disciple is to extend that same initiative to reconciliation at one's own expense into the conflicts of every day.

A full theoretical system to describe what Gandhi, King, and the cloud of witnesses have taught is still to be developed, yet we already see enough to know that the social scene must henceforth be seen in a new light.

Chapter 4

The Fall and Rise of the Just War Tradition

It is odd, when we take the time to stop to think, that for so much of the history of Western thought, Christian and secular, the question of the morality of warfare has attracted so little the careful attention of moral thinkers. People who would think with considerable care about the justification of the death penalty, where the only persons whose life is taken are those who have been convicted (although in some cases wrongly) of major offenses, or persons who would want to study carefully the arguments made for this or that way of arranging for the distribution of income or the ownership of property, have generally not thought as carefully about what it means morally that massive institutions are created by governments for the sole purpose of destroying persons on the other side of a battle line, most of whom can in no way be considered morally responsible for committing the offenses or making the decisions for which their death is supposed to be the punishment.

The facade under which this negligence has been permitted to persist has been the doctrine of the just war. That doctrine has existed from Aristotle to the present and has taken more or less the same shape within various philosophical systems. It has had its ancient Roman forms, its medieval Christian forms, its modern nationalist Christian forms, its fascist forms, and its Marxist forms.

When I say that the just war tradition is a facade, this does not mean that the people who hold to it are insincere, or that

the people who have died and who have killed under the cover
of its justifications were never sincere or noble people. The word
"facade" says more precisely that the tradition, as a construct of
doctrines, presents a surface appearance which is not the same as
what goes on behind the justification which it presents. In order
to make understandable the thesis which I have stated argumen-
tatively to begin with, we shall need to be patient with some systematic definitions and with some historical descriptions.

We therefore return from a description of recent American
social history to a chapter in worldwide intellectual history. The
theory of the just war is as old as Christendom: that is, as old as
the peace which was concluded between the Christian churches
and the Roman Empire in the fourth century. Before that time,
there had been no thought of an alliance between the churches
and Caesar, nor of Caesar's being blessed by the church. Now,
however, that the fate of the regime and that of the faith had
been blessed together, it was understandable that a new morality
was needed.

Before this great transition, the contrast between the Christians
and Caesar's armies was marked by several features. Caesar himself was persecuting the Christians intermittently. Even when
persecution was not raging, the entire Roman enterprise was
idolatrous, with each military unit devoted to the worship of
some god or goddess. At times, Caesar himself demanded that he
be honored as divine. Like the Jews, Christians could not possibly
in good conscience grant such a claim. Life in Caesar's court was
marked by brutality, sexual disorder, falsehood, and intrigue and
was oppressive to its subjects at its best.

To all this was added the simple conviction of Christians that
the shedding of blood was forbidden by divine law. Tertullian had
said it most simply: "in disarming Peter, the Lord has disarmed us
all."[1] Historians desiring to find earlier precedents for Christians'
accepting military service argue that the reason for this early rejection of the army was the idolatry and not the bloodshed. They

---

[1] See Tertullian, *On Idolatry*, chapter 19 in *Ante-Nicene Fathers*, vol. 3 (Grand
Rapids: Eerdmans, 1963).

suggest that if there had been a nonidolatrous Roman army, the bloodshed might have been acceptable. There is no ground in the sources for making that kind of distinction and no basis in historical method for asking a question like that of ancient sources. Before the fourth century, there is no known written expression of Christian thought on the matter indicating that service in Caesar's army was approved of by any writer, bishop, or synod. There was the exercise of patience, permitting a soldier who was converted to Christianity in peacetime to complete his term of service rather than deserting. By approximately A.D. 180, there was also an undefinable number of Christians who did accept military service, provoking denunciations from thinkers like Tertullian. The presence of Christians in the military was no more acceptable than their participation in adultery and idolatry; all three were recognized and denounced by the Fathers.

The church found itself in the Constantinian alliance, and we can see quite simply why the old moral guidelines could not be sufficient. One may detail this change in three dimensions:

a. The sovereign of the empire must himself be welcomed as an agent of divine providence. He is not merely one unique church member whose profession the clergy hesitate to make illegal (just as pastors in some border villages hesitate to challenge the sin of smuggling). He is a special instrument of divine providence. His military successes are demonstrations of grace and must therefore not be immoral.

b. Within the fourth century, everyone except the Jews in the population will be obliged to make public Christian allegiance. Non-Christian faith is no longer a legal possibility. But if everyone is Christian, Christian ethics must be so defined that everyone can do what needs to be done. Morality will then need to be tailored to meet the needs of the social process rather than being derived from the revelation of God in Christ.

c. For these social reasons, we may have a psychological-philosophical reason: it became uncomfortable to think there was a moral obligation that is not equally obligatory for everyone. One comes to think of morality as derived from "nature," which is the same for everyone, rather than from a distinctive covenant which might be different for Jews or for Christians. Concern for philosophical generalizability replaces concern for covenant fidelity as the dominant logic of moral discourse.

Once these adjustments have been made, it is no surprise that it will be possible to find the resources for beginning to describe the duties which apply to rulers in Roman legal thinkers like Cicero. The doctrine of the justifiable war then developed through several gradual phases:

a. In the age of Ambrose and his disciple Augustine, the conception of regrettably justifiable civil violence is present in numerous places in their writings without ever becoming directly the subject of theological attention.
b. In subsequent centuries, efforts to discipline the use of violence are made particularly within the context of the penitential disciplines. Therefore the records are found most frequently in canon law.
c. It is only in the age of Thomas Aquinas that we find major paragraphs of a treatise on moral theology devoted to the possibility that war may be morally justified. In Aquinas we find stated the criteria of *ius ad bellum*: intention, authority, and cause.
d. Still later, these two streams of the tradition are interlocked with a third, namely, civil law, to develop further a corpus of *ius in bello*, permitting and prohibiting specific strategies and weapons.
e. In the age of Hugo Grotius there begins to develop a corpus of international law, transposing the same general principles from the realm of moral theology to that of diplomacy and international arbitration.

The moral strength of the just war tradition can be summarized as follows: when fully understood, it set aside the notion that war may be morally desirable, "holy" because it was commanded by God. From the age of Augustine until the end of the Crusades, this distinction was not made. Some wars were justified because God commanded them and others because of a properly political cause. By the end of the Middle Ages, on the other hand, the two categories came to be distinguished. The holy war model, drawn from the days of Joshua, represented by the Christian Crusade and the Muslim jihad, increasingly came to be seen as a logically different phenomenon. On the other hand, the justifiable war needed to have a finite political cause, to be a matter of last resort, to be winnable, and to be fought in such a way as to respect the moral rights of the adversary.

The second, other unworthy mode of thought which the just war position set aside was Machiavellian "realism": the notion that the laws in wartime ceased to speak (*leges silent*). Just as Machiavelli denied the existence of any morality binding the behavior of a sovereign toward either his subjects or his adversaries, so also this cynical view denies that there is any point to moral or legal discourse once one resorts to the arbitrament of arms. The just war tradition, classically represented by the prolegomena to Grotius' *Laws of War*,[2] insists that although ordinary rules of international relations have broken down and domestic law may be suspended for the emergency, war itself continues to be a political transaction subject to rules. When held to honestly, the just war tradition is morally important because it rejects the holy war and it rejects cynical realism. It articulates restraints which must be observed.

When this body of tradition was first developed, it was thought of as applying only to a very small group of people. For example, a prince and his knights might carry on a just combat. He might conscript his peasant subjects for a limited period of time, but they would hardly be good fighters. He might hire mercenaries, but he could not afford many. Thus, most Christians

---

[2] Although it is possible that Yoder is referring to Hugo Grotius' *The Law of War and Peace*, trans. Louise R. Loomis (New York: Walter J. Black, 1949), at this point, it is much more likely that he intends to point to Grotius' *Prolegomena to the Law of War and Peace*, trans. Francis W. Kelsey (Indianapolis, Ind.: Bobbs-Merrill, 1957).

remained under the moral obligations of nonviolence. Not only religious penitents but peasants and tradesmen were also exempted from combat.

Thus the area covered by the authorization of limited violence was very restrained in terms of the number of people for whom it was morally permissible to kill. Even for these people, the deed was not looked on as righteous. It called for penitence even when the blood was shed in a just cause. Further, it was within the authority of bishops to place certain persons or places under the "Peace of God" or to declare a "Truce of God" covering certain times so that the priority of domestic peace over conflict could be protected.

Simply because the doctrine stated in its ideal form has a certain moral integrity, I do not affirm that it is theologically acceptable from a biblical or ecumenical or contemporary perspective. Its initial logical integrity may, however, serve as a point of orientation to permit us to discern the decline of the doctrine, a decline which has been going on ever since early modern times.

The Protestant Reformation and the Fall of the Tradition[3]

The Protestant Reformers certainly had no intention of innovating in the field of social morality. Yet, unintentionally, the meaning of the doctrine changed in their hands for a number of reasons:

a. Whereas for Catholic teachers the doctrine was a matter of unexamined consensus, for the Protestants, it is written into the creeds. A Catholic may be nonviolent, may affirm a pacifism of principle and not be a heretic; a Lutheran or an Anglican or a Presbyterian cannot.
b. The Protestant Reformation redefines the relationship of church and state. The bishop can no longer reprimand the prince as his son in the church; penitential disciplines have

---

[3] It is interesting to note that this is the only lecture in which Yoder provides subheadings.

been done away with, and the office of the bishop is now subject to the good pleasure of the prince.

c. Religious affiliation is now not only subject to modification by the rule of civil order (*cujus region, ejus religio*), but it is also a matter about which it is possible to wage war.

d. The exempt categories of penitents and religious are done away with, as well as the morality of "evangelical counsels" to which the more devoted people would be invited voluntarily to commit themselves.

The Renaissance and the Enlightenment likewise weakened the capacity of the doctrine to provide moral restraint. The authority of clergy who occasionally used to be able to proclaim a truce or to mediate a peace was undercut. The very notion of transcendent moral standards governing human behavior by right began to be replaced by the conviction that men could calculate, in their own wisdom, what needs to be done toward what ends. The cynical opportunism of princes like those described by Machiavelli was in no way new, but now it was newly possible to make a philosophical case for opportunism. The concepts of just authority and just cause, and especially those of just means, are debunked as never having really described the way decisions were made.

Still more sweepingly, the credit of the just war tradition was undermined by the development of the modern state, with its claim to unqualified sovereignty based not on delegation from some higher government (to say nothing of divine mandate) but simply by the fact of its existence. The idealism of a Grotius, which constructs a set of rules by which sovereign nations would govern their relations to one another, was entertained as long as it was in the national interest and was abandoned cynically whenever it was more profitable. The notion of national sovereignty became even more anarchic when with the age of revolution it was "the people" for whom that absolute moral autonomy was claimed rather than the king. Now that claim is multiplied by the temptation it lays before demagogues. A king who has become involved in a war which turns unprofitable can stop fighting when his money runs out; a "democratic" nation may discover that the people have been urged into such a militant spirit that their leaders must fight on beyond bankruptcy into utter defeat. This happened on both sides in World War I.

Once the nation has begun to be glorified as an absolute, the way is open for war to become "total" in several meanings of that term. We speak of a war as "total" in that it is waged by the entire population, not only by soldiers. The entire economy is mobilized for military production. Winning or losing may be less a matter of success on the battlefield than of maintaining or losing economic momentum. It is total in the sense of human jeopardy: new weapons make everyone a victim or hostage, and render utopian the notion of noncombatant immunity. It may become total as well in the sense that one party demands unconditional surrender or even the renunciation of natural sovereignty of the other, while the just war tradition had sought only the restoration of a more just and defensible peace. It may become "total" in that the understanding of the authority behind their cause authorizes some belligerents to abandon restraint in the interest of victory at any cost, or even causes continuing hostility beyond the possibility of victory because of some notion that to go down fighting in a lost cause is more heroic than to sue for peace.

In all of these respects, what happens with the totalization of war is that, instead of living up to the theological definition of the justifiable war, it becomes again what the just war doctrine intended to reject, namely, a crusade or a "cynical realistic" war in which the adversaries have no rights and there is no effective commitment to restraint.

The Rise of the Tradition

It is perhaps too soon to speak literally, as my title suggests, of a renewal of the just war tradition in its original moral intention. We have yet to see a situation where the affective, consistent application of the doctrine leads an entire Christian community, a church body, or her accountable theologians into a firm position of refusal to obey and to support a war effort to which their national government calls them. We are, however, progressing visibly in that direction. It is the early stages of that progress we do well to note as follows:

a. It was already visible after the wars of the age of Napoleon that the "total" character which war had taken on had gone beyond the bounds of moral accountability. Artists like Goya and storytellers like Victor Hugo (and of course Tolstoy) made this judgment more clear than the theologians could. The Crimean War, by its uselessness, and the American Civil War, by its destructiveness, reinforced this awareness. So it was that in 1869, the bishops gathering in Rome for the First Vatican Council prepared for their working agenda the possibility of a declaration condemning modern war as intrinsically no longer subject to the bounds of proportionality and discrimination. Of course, the initial preoccupation of the council with the issue of defining papal infallibility and the council's early termination due to the outbreak of war kept that topic from coming to discussion.

b. There was overwhelming agreement, after 1918, that the Great War had imposed monstrously greater sacrifices on the peoples of Europe and America than could ever be justified by its initial pretexts. A cry of condemnation arose against arms merchants and others accused of fostering war for reasons based on their own selfish interest. Wide public resentment supported two decades of disarmament treaties and negotiations as well as the early efforts of the League of Nations. But in none of this ultimately fruitless struggle was it the case that Christians or anyone else had occasion to look more closely at the just war logic. If (as they hoped) we are deciding not to have any more wars at all, by virtue of an act of political will, then the complicated set of criteria whereby the tradition had proposed to distinguish between justifiable and unjustifiable causes and means had become unimportant. In fact, the rise of the idea that it would be possible to have a world without war at all also increased the possibility of considering it a just cause that one nation or all the nations might, by means of war, impose "peace" on others.

c. The first serious thinking about the possibility of condemning the specific means of warfare to be used in World War
II was done in an exploratory way by a few individuals in the
1930s. John Ford, a Jesuit moral theologian, in an article written in 1944, first gave wider attention to a question raised by
a lone graduate student in a 1934 dissertation arguing that
the massive bombing of cities could not possibly be morally acceptable.[4] However one might redefine conceptions
of double effect and the "quasicombatant workforce," there
would always be a sizable number of formally and completely
innocent people in any city, people whom a massive bombing could not avoid killing directly and intentionally. There
was public debate on this theme in Great Britain during the
war, but there was no great clarification by theologians. After
the shock of Hiroshima, this position began to gain ground
seriously, although irregularly. One wave of concern arose
around 1955 when it had become clear that the possession
of atomic weapons was no longer an American monopoly. In
this period, a commission of the World Council of Churches
assigned to study "Christians and the Prevention of War in
an Atomic Age" came up with the first effort to state what
later came to be called "nuclear pacifism" or "just war pacifism."[5] A handful of serious academic writings around 1960
stated that argument without attracting wide attention even
in the churches.

d. Reinforcement of a different kind was enacted through the
war crimes trials organized by the Allies. Persons responsible
for crimes against peace and crimes against laws of war were
summoned for due process and sometimes execution. The
notion was thereby reinforced that the laws of war can be

---

[4] The article to which Yoder refers here is John C. Ford, S.J., "The Morality of
Obliteration Bombing," *Theological Studies* 5, no. 3 (1944): 261–309. The disserta-
tion noted here was John Kenneth Ryan's *Modern War and Basic Ethics* (Milwaukee,
Wis.: Bruce Publishing, 1940).

[5] See Thomas Murray Taylor and Robert S. Bilheimer, *Christians and the Prevention
of War in an Atomic Age: A Theological Discussion* (London: SCM Press, 1961).

implemented, at least in some cases, at the expense of those who failed to disobey an unjust order or who had not recognized proper restraint in the prosecution of war.

e. A further level of renewal of the just war tradition was the conviction of conscience of a small number of young men called to serve in wars which they were convinced were unjust. Already Martin Luther had projected the hypothetical possibility of such a "selective conscientious objection" on the part of a subject or soldier. But only in modern times do we have the reports of individual soldiers in significant numbers believing that they knew enough about what a war was about to have a negative judgment on its legitimacy and believing that the matter was their personal responsibility to the point of costly disobedience. Thousands of American young men took such positions during the Vietnam hostilities. I am not informed concerning other times and places, but I trust their example is not unique. In countries where conscientious objection enjoys no legal protection, we would, of course, hardly hear about such cases.

The increasing number of perspectives from which the thought has arisen that it may be morally mandatory to disobey the order of a war-making authority has not yet effectively curbed the arms race. But it has begun in recent years to increase the seriousness of Christians about their civil responsibility in a way that their governments have noticed.

Yet the rising awareness that it may be morally imperative to disobey a government or that it may be impossible morally to carry on military national defense is only half of the lesson that needed to be learned. The other half of the lesson, which is the element which makes the just war tradition our concern in this discussion context, is that at the same time more reasons are becoming visible for not using armed violence. It is becoming visible that there are other means available which had not been seen before or had not been adequately evaluated.

The just war tradition had always said that recourse to violence is wrong except in a situation of last resort (*ultima ratio*). It is very doubtful that the people who made military and political decisions ever really respected this criterion. Once one has a powerful weapon in hand, the temptation is strong to use it as a *prima ratio* in order not to waste more time and run more risks by using smaller weapons and greater patience. Now, however, the question is not merely one of the honesty of military decision makers deciding prematurely that they have tried everything. It is that people like Gandhi and King have brought to the fore a whole range of new possible instruments of social policy, tools in the struggle for social justice or other morally desirable goals. While costly, these instruments are less destructive and interfere less with the possibility of reconstruction after the conflict than armed violence.

In another lecture, I survey in a very thin way what is becoming a very substantial discipline in the realm of political and social science, analyzing past experience and projecting scenarios for potential future conflicts. King and Gandhi gave wide visibility to a possibility that was always there before but had not been exploited. There had been spontaneous acts of noncooperation with oppression. But there was not a body of theory as to how it should work, no analysis of practice as to what was to be learned from past successes and failures, and no systematic preparation for intentional future strategic engagement.

War with weapons demands enormous investment of wealth and human time and intelligence. Weapons must be created. Great numbers of people must be trained to use them. A few persons must develop strategic understandings of how to deploy them. The case for carrying on social conflict with nonviolent weapons will not be given a fair test if there is not the same readiness to invest wealth, ingenuity, training time, and readiness for mortal risk.

The criterion of last resort is a dimension which applies as well in other ways. There now exist international tribunals. There are many formal and informal means of negotiation when the parties to a conflict, in good faith, wish its resolution and do not seek to use it to destroy one another. The criteria of just intention and last resort, in fact, interlock. If both parties really want peace, there will be no war. If even one party sincerely wants peace, there will be almost no circumstance where a nonmilitary solution, even at great cost, would not be preferable to the judgment of arms.

It is just twenty years ago that Pope John Paul II, responding to the shock wave of fear which had been sent around the world by the American/Soviet confrontation over missiles in Cuba, circulated his encyclical *Peace on Earth* not only to Catholics but to all people of good will.[6] That marked the beginning of carefully structured Catholic appropriation of the "nuclear pacifist" position just described above.

We see here the convergence of two different limits. The top limit of justifiable war, the threshold beyond which destructiveness is so great that its use could never be justified, is increasingly pressing in upon us because of the escalation of the destructiveness, the number of weapons, and the difficulty of their control. The lower threshold of "last resort" is rising, so to speak, in view of the increasing availability of international means of mediation and adjudication and in view of greater awareness of the potential of nonviolent means of struggle. In the American experience, it is fitting that, twenty years later, the council of bishops prepared a pastoral letter moving more precisely and courageously in this direction than had ever been the case before. Just this month, the bishops met in Chicago to review the third draft of their pastoral letter: "The Challenge of Peace: God's Promise and Our Response."[7]

---

[6] The document to which Yoder refers here is *Pacem in Terris*. See David J. O'Brien and Thomas A. Shannon, eds., *Catholic Social Thought: The Documentary Heritage* (Maryknoll, N.Y.: Orbis, 1992), 129–62.

[7] The final text was later published, in 1983, as "The Challenge of Peace: God's Promise and Our Response." See O'Brien and Shannon, eds., *Catholic Social Thought*, 492–571.

Chapter 5

The Science of Conflict

Most of the analysis which needs to be brought to bear upon the problem of war as a "theological" issue is theological in the narrow sense; that is, it needs to ask about Scriptures and tradition or about how the will of God is revealed and interpreted within the community of faith. Christians have differed about those issues in ways that need to be studied in their own terms, and that is the main theme of my lectures. It is, however, no less the case that those debates about moral theology intersect with other debates about human nature and the shape of society. We cannot discuss theology alone. We must constantly interlock with the human sciences, which are talking about the same phenomena from other perspectives. If the believer says that faith in Jesus Christ makes it possible to love one's enemy, is this not something that could be described by the psychologist? If love leads one to go out and make peace with one's adversary, is this not an event which a sociologist could describe? When a preacher proclaims a phrase like "On violence there is no blessing" (Auf der Gewalt ruht kein Segen[1]), is this not a claim which the historian could verify or refute? It is thus appropriate in fleshing out the realism of the message of reconciliation that we give recognition to the importance

[1] Kurt Scharf (1902–1990), a bishop of the Evangelical Church of Berlin-Brandenburg, made such a statement in sermons and lectures. Scharf was known in Poland for his efforts at German-Polish reconciliation.

of those disciplines. There is no room here for a kind of dualism which would avoid such cross-references on the grounds that they would represent unbelief or a confusion of categories.

Some of the scholarly research in this area has been done by people of pacifist conviction in order to demonstrate that renouncing violence does not mean abandoning concern for the course of public events. Others are quite independent of such ideological commitment, and they see conflict processes as an especially challenging object of sociological analysis.

The beginnings of sociology as an empirical discipline tended to use models of stability or equilibrium, comparing a society to a human body with every organ working well, to a peaceable village with everyone in his place, or to a balanced market with all needs being met. That approach had value. It committed people to interpret social events as efforts of the social organism as a whole or of member groups within it to restore the balance when it had been distorted. Increasingly, however, social observers of all philosophical schools are finding it more constructive and instructive to describe disequilibrium and conflict as realities in their own right rather than as a phase along the way to restored balance. That way, one sees better how a society has numerous centers of decision and initiative and numerous definitions of what a just equilibrium would be.

Hand in hand with this development of sociology as a descriptive science, a parallel development has emerged with regard to the kinds of analysis and skills which are appropriate for interpreting and directing social and political action. Here, too, it is more appropriate to say that we have a conflict which needs to be "managed," in a way that takes account of the valid interests and human dignity of all parties, rather than to maintain the notion of a peaceable order which had almost been established and which needs only to be completed or renewed against the resistances of those who would disturb it.

This shift from models of organic unity to models of intergroup conflict has several values for peace theology. It will interpret and contribute to the development of techniques of conflict management which can respond more effectively and economically to the injustices and needs for which it was thought in the past that only violence is a possible recourse. To say it in the terms of the old just war tradition, even when a cause is just and the authority pursuing it is legitimate, violence is only justified when it is, in reality, the very last resort. If we can see that there are more alternative instruments of change toward justice available than had been thought about, then this changes the fundamental structure of the moral issue.

Images of the social organism as a unity needing to have but one will, implemented from above, are especially congenial to social systems which endanger the rights of individuals and minorities and which easily reach for violence in the defense of their "peace." The image of society in which diverse groups have diverse interests—many of them justified but some of them more justified than others, and some of them morally unworthy—fits appropriately with the biblical vision of the church in a hostile world, a realistic vision which Christians since the fourth century left behind, much to their loss, because they believed that the kingdom of God could be served by the blessing of human kingdoms.

Not only does this provide a picture of the social world that is more realistic, it also aids us in overcoming the isolation of theology proper from the social world. The Christian doctrines of reconciliation and forgiveness have been thought of for too long as applying directly to the estrangement between God and the individual soul and as related only very indirectly to estrangement between God's creatures.

The language of conversion and reconciliation is laid upon us by the biblical witness, but it should not be understood in a sentimental way. A process of conflict resolution has not failed if one of the parties is less than joyful and wholehearted in accepting a more just arrangement. Often the acceptance of a more just solution is an adjustment which takes time and is assisted by the experience of the new arrangement actually working well. Thinkers about conflict management like Saul Alinsky[2] and

[2] Saul Alinsky (1909–1972) was widely recognized as a pioneer in community organizing in America. His *Rules for Radicals: A Pragmatic Primer for Realistic Radicals*

activists like Danilo Dolci[3] rightly warn against such a preoccupation with the adversary's "conversion" that steps to social amelioration short of conversion are rejected.

The specifically Christian access to the notion of conflict resolution as a visible social process is the guidance given by Jesus to his disciples: "If your brother sins, talk to him privately about it. . . ." The intent of reconciliation is served, not denied, by the most direct confrontation. If need be, the circle must widen: "If he will not listen, take two or three witnesses. . . ."[4] Yet the intent is not victory but restored wholeness and common commitment.

Creative study and theory in this field of "conflict resolution" as a social science is, not surprisingly, interdisciplinary: it creates connections beyond the several provinces of traditional academic specialization. Kenneth Boulding is an economist with very broad competence; Elise Boulding is a sociologist.[5] Anatol Rapoport and Pitirim Sorokin are sociologists of a more philosophical European school.[6] Adam Curle, who pioneered the development of a procedural analysis of how social interactions

---

(New York: Random House, 1971) provided the codified structure for later movements.

[3] See chapter 3, footnote 3.

[4] See Matthew 18:15-16—"If another member of the church sins against you, go and point out the fault when the two of you are alone. If the member listens to you, you have regained that one. But if you are not listened to, take one or two others along with you, so that every word may be confirmed by the evidence of two or three witnesses."

[5] Kenneth Boulding (1910–1993) was a devout Quaker as well as a noted economist. Boulding taught at several universities across America, including the University of Michigan, where he founded the Center for Research in Resolution in 1959. Two years prior, the publication of the *Journal of Conflict Resolution* became the first periodical devoted to the topic, and Boulding was instrumental in its launch. Boulding met his wife, Elise Boulding (1920), at a Quaker meeting. She is an important activist and scholar as well, focusing on the role of women and families in the peace process.

[6] Anatol Rapoport's (1911–2007) principal endeavors were in the field of mathematical biology and general systems theory. He collaborated with Kenneth Boulding in the creation of the *Journal of Conflict Resolution*. Pitirim Sorokin (1889–1968) fled his native Russia to become a sociology professor in America, where his best-known work, *Social and Cultural Dynamics* (1957), revolutionized the study of social change.

go about "making peace," was first a professor of pedagogy.[7] Gene Sharp began the second generation of such studies with *Politics of Nonviolent Action*, a dissertation in the realm of political science and government.[8] James Laue is an urban sociologist.[9] Other strong contributions are made by social psychologists.

The work of these researchers has taken root especially in the last decades in public and private universities and research institutes, linked together by the International Peace Research Association.[10] Like any young discipline, it is marked by debates about its limits and methods and about the relations between scientific honesty, value commitment, and technical competence. All that I can do in this context is chart the terrain which this new set of sciences is surveying.

The background for a revision of sociology is appropriately a revision of history. Our capacity to interpret what is happening here and now is assisted, and may be hampered by, our understandings of what has happened before. Therefore, every renewal of the future demands a vision of the past.

One necessary dimension of such revision—the easiest but perhaps the least productive—is simply to seek to retell a story from the other side. In every war, the winning party writes the history books for the next generation. Soon the third parties of the children of the victims, if the archives have not been

---

[7] Adam Curle (1916–2006), a military veteran of World War II and later a Quaker convert, was a British academic who advocated for nonmilitary conflict resolution as an activist and professor at Harvard University and the Centre for Peace Studies in Bradford, England.

[8] Gene Sharp's (b. 1928) *Politics of Nonviolent Action* was published in three parts. *Power and Struggle: Politics of Nonviolent Action, Part 1* and *Methods of Nonviolent Action: Politics of Nonviolent Action, Part 2* were published in 1973. *Dynamics of Nonviolent Action: Politics of Nonviolent Action, Part 3* was published in 1985. All three parts were published in Boston by Porter Sargent.

[9] James Laue (1937–1993) was selected in 1979 by President Jimmy Carter to establish a national academy to teach peacemaking techniques, an initiative that culminated in the U.S. Institute of Peace in 1984. Laue was working in Memphis alongside Martin Luther King Jr. as a federal mediator when King was assassinated. Laue later served as professor of conflict resolution at George Mason University.

[10] Since 1964 the IPRA has hosted biennial conferences to share interdisciplinary research efforts with an international membership.

destroyed, will find the evidence for seeing things the other way. But that kind of revision is still a part of the old game of letting history be the history of battles, of letting the writing of it be a glorification of one's present regime, and of letting the battle for the right to interpret be part of the battle for sovereignty.

A more fundamental revision will not merely illuminate the same questions from the other side but will ask other questions. Instead of chronicling how ruling dynasties clashed over borders, we will ask how parents raised their children to get along with one another. Instead of interpreting with ever-greater finesse the documents produced by literate minorities, we will ask how illiterate sages communicated to their grandchildren the historical depth of their culture. We may find that water tables, or the level of infestation by rats, or mutations in epidemic-causing microbes, or the discovery by some blacksmith of a new way to sharpen a pruning tool would make more difference to the quality of ordinary human existence than did the conflicts about which ruling house was collecting the taxes.

There is, then, a historiography of violence which, because it chooses to observe primarily those matters, teaches us that the fate of nations is in the hands of their armies. There would also be (and there is beginning to be) a historiography of the community structures of ordinary people which, by looking for other facts, finds other facts. This historiography teaches us that most of the human community's quality is necessarily dependent upon avoiding violence and that truly foundational values are seldom served by those who claim to do it with the sword.

Tolstoy said long ago that progress in history was made by the persecuted.[11] If children grow to fruitful adulthood, if fields become fertile, or if carefully coordinated labor achieves large goals, it will be because ways have been found to hold destructive violence to a minimum. The finding of ways to hold destructive violence to a minimum is the object of sociology and psychology where those two disciplines intersect. There are better ways

[11] Leo Tolstoy, trans. Aylmer Maude, *What I Believe* (New York: Oxford University Press, 1932), 47–48.

and there are worse ways for groups to manage their conflict. The study of how conflict is resolved more or less economically, or more or less destructively, is a descriptive science that challenges the best intelligences to observe and analyze. The actual management of conflict is an applied science derived from those insights. In a healthy society, it may also be a vocational specialization. Between small groups, as in family conflict, or medium-sized groups, as in urban neighborhoods, the record of the professional services of this kind is already impressive. On a larger scale, the study of conflict management merges into the analysis of a kind of nonviolent agency (action) of which I spoke in earlier lectures. On the still-larger scale—namely, on the level of conflicts between nations, or in the defense of the national values of peoples deprived of national autonomy—the experimentation is in its infancy. Yet there is every reason to expect that the lessons to learn will be similar. Therefore, it is a theologically sober projection when we suggest that in the long run (a) the defense of those values which traditionally people have thought they should protect with lethal violence will be more economically and less destructively defended through the use of nonviolent instruments, and (b) the relative advantage of nonviolent means is growing to the same extent that the destructiveness of the available violent instruments is increasing as the controllability of those weapons diminishes.

It may be worthwhile to note in a few paragraphs two internal questions which arise in the different disciplines of psychology and sociology when more attention is given to conflict resolution. In the sociological field, there is the challenge of interpreting the place of aggressivity as a basic component of animal human nature. In psychology, "aggressivity" is also the word used for an ambivalent component of our behavior.

Just in the last generation, we have observed in zoology and anthropology the extension of the interpretation of human nature which accentuates the continuity between man and the rest of the animal kingdom, especially the other primates. Scientists derive from the study of other animals characteristics that are then projected into human nature to throw light on some of the fundamental constants of human nature—if that is what they are.

The scientist whose name is most prominently associated with the development of this subdiscipline is the Austrian zoologist Konrad Lorenz, followed by a wide range of zoologists and zoologically inclined anthropologists in the past fifteen years.[12] "Aggressiveness" is described in Lorenz as a mark of all the kinds of animals that one can study. Aggressiveness is necessary in animal sociology in a defensive way. Animals do not just generally go around biting each other, but they attack one another at certain points. As Lorenz studied them, it became more clear that the points at which they would attack each other were precisely the "territories" that were somehow delimited as their own "turf." This describes a defensive aggressiveness, not an imperialistic drive. Most animals do not have imperialistic drives, although some of the higher primates do try to extend their turf. The generalization is that there is a built-in defensive aggressiveness which is part of nature, part of the necessity of survival according to a Darwinian understanding of viable animal nature. One then extends that to humans. One says that war is a natural expression of something that is unavoidably a part of what it means to be an organism that evolved out of the earlier history of the animal kingdom. It is our nature. Why fight it?

You cannot fight it. You have to accept it. Some people draw antipacifist conclusions from this, saying that the notion of reconciliation and the notion of a wider human community—the idea that you could learn to turn the other cheek from your faith or from Christian education—is antinatural and, therefore, bad or sick. Others would derive alternative conclusions, saying that this just tells us the shape of the problem we have. What we need to do is to find ways to channel our aggressiveness in nondestructive patterns. This part of our nature can either be sublimated or guided fruitfully so that it will apply to enemies other than individual human beings and to causes other than

[12] Konrad Lorenz (1903–1989) published in a variety of genres, and the text to which Yoder seems to refer here is *On Aggression* (New York: Harcourt, Brace, 1966).

just defending our own turf. We can then accept this reading of human constitution and still not be drawn away from a pacifist application.

With regard to conflict in sociology, I already said that the answer of the Christian peace message is not to dichotomize or to reject worldly wisdom but to incorporate it in the promise of global reconciliation. Similarly, we must say with regard to this animal-anthropological vision that it cannot ultimately be alien to the peace that God gives. Some components of basic animal aggressivity may be seen as fallen and destructive; others are fundamentally wholesome and ready to be used in giving power and structure to the reconstitution of human community. There is nothing to fear in the encounter with improved information on this dimension of human nature.

The other cross-disciplinary encounter relates to the psychological disciplines. Aggressiveness is a part of the nature of the individual, as personality theory discerns this, or as the counseling professions inductively tells us what our nature is. A person who does not have an aggressive will is a sick person. You must be self-affirming. You must therefore push at the borders between your personality and your neighbor's. If you completely internalize all your mother's pressures on you to be nice, to give in, and not to offend people, this will, in the long run, keep you from growth into responsible maturity. Too much emphasis at the wrong time on giving in to others and loving your enemies is itself psychologically dangerous. It will undercut the growth of normal, wholesome self-affirmation in the personality.

It is possible to interpret a nonviolent ethical commitment in such a way as to make it contradictory to wholesome personality development or expression. Now how does that relate to the rest of what we have been talking about? It would then be possible, obviously, for certain kinds of teaching, especially teaching about nonresistance (perhaps contrasted at this point with teaching about nonviolent action) to have a stultifying effect on personality and development. Does it have to have that effect? I do not see why. There would certainly be times when to be consciously nonresistant, to say nothing of being active nonviolently in a studied way, requires more personality, self-awareness, self-control, self-understanding, self-acceptance, than just to run along with a conflict that has been structured for you in a brutal way.

Just as was said twice before (once with regard to the sociology of conflict and again with regard to the anthropology of aggressivity), the disciplines concerned with the psychic wholeness of the individual should also be welcome allies in the development of a theological perspective on human peace. There is no clash between psychic wholeness and love of the enemy. To love the enemy is not masochism nor self-hatred but the widest kind of self-acceptance, the most inclusive way to receive one's self as a gift from God and share that selfhood with one's fellow creatures who are no less loved and gifted by God.

Chapter 6

From the Wars of Joshua to Jewish Pacifism

The topic of biblical resources for Christian thinking about peace is one of those where we have become accustomed to thinking that little is to be gained from the text of the Bible itself. We assume that what it has to say is already well known and is insufficient. We believe we already know that the Old Testament teaches a kind of nationalism which cannot be a model for us and that the New Testament teaches a kind of pacifism which cannot be a model either. Therefore, Christian thinking on these matters has, especially since the fourth century, been concerned with finding other sources in nature, reason, or custom to give guidance to the extent that it is possible to think morally at all about matters of war and peace. We continue to see the Bible used as a mine for general slogans about the broad peacemaking purposes of God—which have their place in celebrations and sermons—but we no longer assume that serious and specific moral guidance could be found in the Scriptures.

This assumption is mistaken. In a more extended and more academic treatment, it would be appropriate that I should converse critically with the traditional developments which have led to that widely accepted consensus: the contributions of Neoplatonism, Germanic tribalism, and Roman understandings of civil order would have to be identified. But for our purposes, it must suffice to restate the simple affirmation that the postcritical reading of the Scriptures still has something to teach us about national loyalty and the outsider, about God and our enemies.

The shape of the question put to us by the phenomenon of the wars of YHWH has been determined for many of us by the dualism of Peter of Chelcic and Tolstoy.[1] In the age of Moses and Joshua, war was morally obligatory; now Jesus tells us it was wrong. From that simple beginning, one can move in two directions. One can say that we simply stand with Jesus, and in rejecting those particular portions of the Old Testament we radically relativize all of the Hebrew backgrounds of the Christian faith. Then we will have a smaller Bible to guide us, and we shall be permanently embarrassed by the fact that the New Testament itself generally assumes rather than rejects the authority of the Old. Subsequent experience has demonstrated, as well, that such an attitude can lead to unevangelical anti-Semitism.

The other approach is to say that when Jesus set aside the model of Moses and Joshua he did so only for certain realms of life, either only within the church or only for the level of face-to-face relationships, while letting the legitimacy of war stand unchanged for nations and their rulers and for those whom the rulers call to serve them. Since God commanded wars then, war cannot be sinful now.

In both approaches, the argument is legalistic. Neither interpretation places the matter in the concrete historical context of the Ancient Near East nor in the narrative framework in which the Hebrew Scriptures themselves reported.

Beginning with the pamphlet of Gerhard von Rad, a sizable accumulation of scholarly analysis has improved our understanding of the wars of YHWH.[2] The scholars differ in significant ways but agree on most of what I shall be reporting here. That YHWH is a warrior is the theme of the song of Miriam, which from a literary-critical perspective may be one of the oldest texts.

---

[1] Peter, also known as Petr Chelčický (A.D. 1390–1460), was an early Bohemian pacifist writer whose work influenced later Anabaptists and Quakers.

[2] Gerhard von Rad (1901–1971) pioneered the study of the oral sources and traditions behind the text of the Old Testament. Yoder later collaborated with Marva Dawn in the translation and publication of von Rad's *Holy War in Ancient Israel* (Eugene, Ore.: Wipf and Stock, 1990).

The salvation of the Israelites at the Red Sea is celebrated as the battle won by YHWH of Hosts.

All of the gods of the peoples were warriors. Each god defended his own nation. The prosperity or the misfortune of the nation demonstrated the power or the weakness of their god. The identity of Israel is defined at the outset by the liberating acts of their patron.

In order to understand its distinctive message about God as creator and provider, the way to read the first chapter of Genesis is not to compare it to the accounts which the geologist or biologist gives of the origin of the earth or the species, but to compare it with the other Near Eastern cosmogonies. For the same reason, the way to read the accounts of YHWH's wars is not to find in them a comparison to the wars of our time but to contrast them to the other religious justifications of domination in their own epoch. It is those elements of originality which will progressively define for us a specifically Israelite understanding of YHWH as different from the gods of the nations.

It is YHWH himself who gives the victory. It is not that the Israelites do a better job than their enemies of deploying their forces or that they have better weapons; it is YHWH himself who gives the victory. In the most dramatic cases, which critical interpretation suspects may also be the most original, the Israelites do not fight at all. That was the case for the Red Sea, for Jericho, for Gideon, for Jehoshaphat. In other cases, the Israelites participated in the battle or "came to the aid of YHWH," but it was not their contribution which was decisive.

The contribution of the faithful Israelite is, therefore, not to fight boldly and even less to fight brutally; it is to trust YHWH. This trust includes the renunciation of alliances with other pagan powers or the use of their military technology (horses and chariots).

The protection of YHWH cannot be presumed to apply to the interests of an Israelite nation or a Davidic royal house if the demands of the covenant are not fulfilled. Israel does not possess YHWH. In the case of disobedience or idolatry, the Israelites will find YHWH as their enemy, with Assyria or Cyrus serving as God's scourge.

The holy wars end with the creation of the Davidic state. Judges and Samuel contain some texts which describe that adoption of kingship as a betrayal of YHWH's lordship and an institution of tyranny, while other texts describe it as authorized by YHWH. Even the more affirmative texts describe a model of kingship with a set of traits that does not fit the real experience of Israel at all. "He must not get horses from Egypt, nor increase his wives or his gold and silver. He must copy and study the Law."[3]

However we resolve the difficulty of interpreting how and whether God accepted kingship, it is clear that the nature of war changed with David. There are now standing armies whose officers are foreign professionals, like Uriah the Hittite. The taxation which supports them and the splendor of the royal palace is responsible for new oppression. From now on, if wars are won, it is by virtue of the shrewdness and the strength of Israel's soldiers. From now on, we no longer find the rhetoric or rites of a just war after the model of Joshua and Gideon. If there is language like that, it is with the report that YHWH has taken the other side.

This account has two kinds of importance for later Christian thinking about the morality of violence. The first line of relationship is to the perennial debate about the morality of violence in which a kind of negative legalism has said that since God commanded those wars back then, war must not be wrong in principle. Yet the closer we look at the wars which were reported to be commanded back then, the more we see that they are unique, occasional happenings, miracles, and sacrifices, but they are in no way comparable to war as a regular institute of national policy. Only if wars today were commanded by prophets and won by miracles would the wars of YHWH be a pertinent example. As it is, they count on the other side. Israel was to trust YHWH for

---

[3] Deuteronomy 17:16-19—"Even so, he must not acquire many horses for himself, or else his heart will turn away; also silver and gold he must not acquire in great quantity for himself. When he has taken the throne of his kingdom, he shall have a copy of this law written for him in the presence of the levitical priests. It shall remain with him and he shall read it in all the days of his life, so that he may learn to fear the Lord his God, diligently observing all the words of this law and these statutes."

national salvation rather than using other rational and technical instruments like alliances with Egypt or the accumulation of forces. It is inappropriate to read those ancient stories as a document on whether war is sin, because that is not what they are meant to be documenting. What they were documenting is that YHWH takes the side of his people so that they can trust him for their continued existence. If that fundamental truth has any relationship to later times and to the New Testament community, it is precisely in the direction of trusting God for survival rather than the lesser-evil arguments for war.

A second level of relevance is the light that this Old Testament story must have thrown on the way Jesus and his audiences likely would have looked at their decisions. We tend to assume (because we have been told it) that in the gospel accounts about Jesus he is shown recommending patterns of behavior that only make sense if you believe the world is coming to an end. So the call of Jesus to love the enemy and renounce self-defense is usually written off as absolute idealism, as apolitical withdrawal, intelligible only if the society's future has been written off. Either Jesus is practical, and then he will have to admit a certain amount of sin and violence, or he is idealistic and calls for people to behave in a way not possible in the real world. But the audience to whom Jesus spoke was people who had in their Scriptures other accounts of deliverance.

The picture is different if Jesus' listeners' minds were authentically formed by the stories of divine salvation in the Old Testament experience. Those who were "waiting for the consolation of Israel" might very well have seen in those stories a model for the way God would save his people again. When Jesus used the language of liberation, proclaiming the restoration of the kingdom community and a new pattern of life, without predicting or authorizing or undertaking any violent means to bring about those ends, he would not have seemed to be a dreamer to his listeners. He could simply have been seen in the succession of Jehoshaphat and Hezekiah, expecting that once more the believing people would be saved despite their weakness, on condition that they "be still and wait to see the salvation of YHWH" (Exod

14:3). Having that expectation in the back of their minds throws
a special light on what might have been thought by the hearers of
the "kingdom inauguration discourse" of Luke 4 or the Sermon
on the Plain of Luke 6.

The modern reader is stopped by the seeming impossibility
of any such event within history as a generalized jubilee (Luke
4:19), nor can one easily imagine "being perfect as your father is
perfect."

The reader then assumes that Jesus must not have been trying
to say what he says, and the mind of the modern interpreter goes
down the paths of paradoxical or symbolic or spiritualist interpretation. On the other hand, for the first hearers of Jesus, the question of whether it was possible could not have gotten in the way of
the promise. They already believed a history in which the impossible had happened. They could hear the promise without filtering
it through the grid of their sense of the limits of the possible.

The sense in which the coming of the kingdom is conceivable
for modern listeners seems to be "off the edge" of the real world,
yet the believing listeners to Jesus remembered the saving events
which had taken place within their own history and on their own
Palestinian soil. A host of modern interpreters of Jesus come to
his proclamation considering it as implying a necessary end of
real history, yet saving wonders had been present in Israel's history through the centuries, as reported in Judges and Chronicles.
Jesus' listeners were not as bothered as we are with the fear that
the coming of the kingdom which he announced might not
happen in reality; they had seen such events before. If they had
doubts, it was in the opposite direction: they would not want that
kind of kingdom to come because of its claims upon them.

My point here is not to discuss, as a theme in critical gospel
interpretation, exactly what Jesus meant or whether what Jesus
meant is credible to modern post-Enlightenment Europeans. I
am asking whether the proclamation of Jesus was intrinsically
credible when it was first spoken. On that subject, the memory
of the miraculous deliverances in Israelite experience—which constituted the primary historical memory of Jesus' audience—would
seem to be nearly conclusive, affirmative evidence.

But the theme for today is not the teaching of Jesus but the continuing evolution of the self-understanding of biblical Israel. Centuries of Christian anti-Semitism have established the pattern of thinking that Jewish faith is warlike and Jesus is peaceable, so that Jesus' announcing a peaceable kingdom was the reason that "the Jews" rejected him. That misreading is a source of continuing confusion in Christian thought. It is made all the more confusing when we remember that Christians, at least since the fourth century, have not been peaceable at all, whereas Jews have never been violent from the second century until this one. In proper historical reorientation, the reading of the first two centuries would be profoundly different from the standard anti-Semitic reading.

Holy wars and divinely sponsored kingship are the beginning and not the end of the Jewish national story. That story moves ahead so that, by the time of the writing of Chronicles, the model is nonviolent salvation after the style of the stories of Jehoshaphat. Ezra and Nehemiah restore the worshipping presence of Jews in Judea under the protection of God without political sovereignty. As Ezra set out from Babylon to return to Jerusalem, we read:

> Then I proclaimed a fast there, at the river Ahava
> that we might humble ourselves before our God
> to seek from his a straight way . . . ,
> for I was ashamed to ask the king for men,
> soldiers and horsemen to protect us
>   against the enemy on our way;
> since we told the king,
> "the hand of our God is for good
>   upon all that seek Him,
> and the power of His wrath
>   is against all that forsake Him."
> So we fasted and besought our God for this,
> and He listened to our entreaty.[4]

[4] Ezra 8:21-23–"Then I proclaimed a fast there, at the river Ahava, that we might deny ourselves before our God, to seek from Him a safe journey for ourselves, our

This redefinition of national community without kingship or national sovereignty is not a counsel of weakness. It is the culmination of the prophetic critique which, from the very beginning, had been addressed to kingship as an inappropriate way to be the people of YHWH. The critique which was an undertone in the stories of Judges and Samuel becomes increasingly clear as the prophets go on. By the time of Isaiah, it called for formal renunciation of politics and diplomacy as usual, alliances with Egypt, and the modernization of military technology. By the time of Jeremiah, it had come to mean the renunciation of statehood and the acceptance of diaspora as the natural way to live. Jeremiah's letter to the exiled community in Babylon calls for them to take their being scattered among the nations as normal. Promises of early national restoration are denounced as lying dreams. The prophets who make such promises were not sent by YHWH:

> Build houses and live in them
> plant gardens and eat their produce.
> Take wives and have sons and daughters;
> take wives for your sons
> and give your daughters in marriage,
> that they may bear sons and daughters;
> multiply there, and do not decrease.
> Seek the welfare of the city where I have sent you into exile,
> and pray to YHWH on its behalf,
> for in its welfare you will find your welfare.[5]

---

children, and all our possessions. For I was ashamed to ask the king for a band of soldiers and cavalry to protect us against the enemy on our way, since we had told the king that the hand of our God is gracious to all who seek him, but his power and his wrath are against all who forsake him. So we fasted and petitioned our God for this, and he listened to our entreaty."

[5] Jeremiah 29:5-7—"Build houses and live in them; plant gardens and eat what they produce. Take wives and have sons and daughters; take wives for your sons, and give your daughters in marriage, that they may bear sons and daughters; multiply there, and do not decrease. But seek the welfare of the city where I have sent you into exile, and pray to the Lord on its behalf, for in its welfare you will find your welfare."

The dominant history of Judaism is the history founded by the message of Jerusalem. From then on, Babylon, more than Palestine, has been the base of the continuing story. The attempt at restoration under Ezra and Nehemiah is not reported as a success. The violent national uprisings of the Maccabees succeeded even less: their stories are not in the Hebrew canon and were not understood by the rabbis as having taken place under the blessing of God. The Zealot adventures of Menachem in A.D. 66–70 and of Bar Kochba in A.D. 132–135 are not seen as the continuation of a faithful community but as mistakes which God judged. Rabbinic communities, as established literally in the Mishnah, are the prolongation of the social form projected by the message of Jeremiah. After 70 and definitely after 135, there is no more interest in solutions following either the Herodian, Sadducean, or the Zealot model.

Two kinds of Jews survive into later history: the Jews who were convinced that in Jesus the Messiah had come and were henceforth called Christians, and the others who gathered around the rabbis. Even within Palestine, Jews lived in a sociology of dispersion without any need for kingship or sovereignty, heirs of the arrangement established by Jochanan ben Zakkai when he disassociated himself from the Zealots.[6] The numerically dominant Jewish identity was for centuries that which was defined from Babylon. The Babylonian community was five centuries old when the generation of Jochanan abandoned the Zealots and almost six centuries old when the generation of Akiva finally accepted that lesson. Christians who, in order to understand Jesus, think that they should take either the Zealots or the Sadducees as representative Jews thereby misread both the Jewish canon and real Jewish history.

Not only did Judaism as defined since Jeremiah forsake their visions of kingship and sovereignty for the historical present under his prophetic guidance, they also forsook violence. The rabbinic corpus is by its nature complex and contradictory. Some

[6] Jochanan ben Zakkai founded the Academy of Jamnia with the blessing of the Roman emperor Vespasian after the rabbi refused to collaborate with the Zealots in violent rebellion. These events took place between A.D. 60 and 70.

passages reject violence completely, even in self-defense; others retain the memory of a judicial system qualified to punish people and of limited wars, since such wars were recorded in ancient histories. But the guidance given by the rabbis for the moral life of the ongoing Jewish community calls for a fundamentally non-violent style of life, even under persecution, on grounds not of strategy or weakness but because that is now seen to be the will of God.

That model of Jewish pacifism was sustained through the Middle Ages after the Christians had made their alliance with the Caesars and continued to be held until our century. Paradoxically, it was the Jews who through all those centuries most faithfully represented within Europe the defenseless style of morality which Jesus had taught. Their ways of explaining that stance were multiple:

a. Blood is sacred. Blood is the life and belongs to God. Even the blood of an animal must not be shed except in a ritual context. The shedding of the blood of a fellow human being is the fundamental denial of human dignity (Genesis 4) from which all other sins against society are derived. Those points in the Old Testament where exception can be made to the wrongness of shedding of blood are in the context of the Mosaic provisions for civil administration or the holy war narratives and *at the most* would apply in a preexile Jewish state. Even there, however, they would not apply rigorously if such a Jewish state had not gone into exile, because Judaism assumes an evolutive process moving toward greater grace and humaneness.

b. The Messiah has not yet come. If anyone could have a right to restore the patterns of vengeance, which alone could justify the shedding of blood, it would be the Messiah. Yet we know that when he comes there will be a time of peace. If the time of his coming will be a time of peace, then we participate in that coming while living already in peace to the extent that we can. For some Jews, living at peace is a part of contributing to his coming.

c. Judaism is marked by the concern to learn properly the lessons from the Zealot experience. This experience came to its final catastrophe in 132–135 with Bar Kochba, but the earlier catastrophe in 66–70 and the still-earlier Maccabean drama all represented the same strategy, and all failed. All but the last failed, at least in part, because *when* the Zealots took power they were unable to bring about the righteous and peaceful community they had promised after all. If anything is constitutive of Rabbinic Judaism, in the sense in which historians speak of it as beginning after 70 or after 135, it is the concern to be clear about having learned the lesson of the wrongness of the Zealot path which God evidently has not blessed. In not blessing the Zealot path, God is telling us something which he has had to tell us more than once.

d. The wisdom in which God presides over the affairs of the *goyim* is not revealed to us in any simple way. We know that he rules over the whole universe and therefore also over all the nations. But the *way* he rules over the nations is not the same as the way he rules over us through the revealed Torah. Therefore, he forbids us to draw immediate conclusions about which things going on in that wider world are of his doing and which are rebellion against him. Since he has given us no clue as to his judgments in those matters, it would be the height of presumptuousness for us to seek to be the instruments of his wrath, to say nothing of doing what we think he must want done ahead of the Messiah's coming.

e. Suffering has a place in the divine economy. That the faithful must suffer is a mystery not yet clear in the Jewish understanding of history. On the one hand, there is a correlation between disobedience and consequent punishment and between obedience and resulting prosperity: if we suffer, we must have disobeyed. Therefore, we should not defend ourselves. Yet this linkage is not automatic, because sometimes the evil ones prosper. Sometimes the suffering of God's people is beyond explanation. Only those who know less of the past think that the drama of Auschwitz has brought this problem to the surface for the first time. In any case, *some* suffering at the hands of the *goyim* is to be accepted as "Sanctifying the Name" of God.

The answers are varied, yet most of them agree in denying that it is in the hands of the faithful to prevent their suffering or to get vengeance by taking up arms themselves. Sometimes the thought is that we are being punished for our sins. To ward off the suffering would be to interfere with God's chastisement. At other times, the suffering is thought of as discipline or training or refining of the spirit rather than as punishment, but again it would be wrong to prevent it. Whichever the explanation would be, our suffering is within the framework of God's sovereign control of events. Since he lets these things happen, we should not prevent them.

The confluence of all these considerations made the global experience of being Jewish in the Middle Ages consistent and convincing. The stance was viable because between pogroms there were stretches of tolerance during which there were some safe niches in society for such a minority. It was self-reinforcing and convincing because the crude, violent, semipagan, tribal culture of their "Christian" oppressors was living proof of the moral superiority of Judaism.

European and American Christianity are far from completing the penance called for by the use of official anti-Semitism in the interest of national and ethnic selfishness. One part of the overdue rehabilitation should be the recognition of the power and of the profound theological rootage of Jewish nonviolence through the centuries.

Chapter 7

Jesus and Nonviolent Liberation

As we seek to understand the nonviolence of Jesus, we will do well to set aside some of the questions that tend to be debated the most—questions which, however, lead the argument away from the heart of the issue.

We should first set aside the question which was given classical shape by Leo Tolstoy: are we to take literally the words of Jesus on the Sermon on the Mount which tell us not to resist the evil person and to love the enemy? Tolstoy's interpretation represented a dramatic narrowing of the question. He set aside problems of general literary interpretation in favor of the simple meaning of the text. He centered on just one text instead of the larger context. He centered upon the moral discourses of Jesus to the neglect of his other teachings and the narrative of his life . . . . That dramatic selectivity has powerful value for some purposes, but it also provokes serious misunderstandings and defense mechanisms which we do well to avoid.

We shall also set aside the negative counterpart of Tolstoy: a kind of antilegalism which says that Jesus must not have been completely opposed to all kinds of violence, since there were soldiers whom he dealt with lovingly without making an issue of their prohibited profession and because he himself used a piece of cord to move animals out of the temple square. Likewise, we do well to set aside discussion of the complex critical questions having to do with the difference between the way the canonical gospel account reads and the original events behind that account. The editorial perspective of Luke is different from that of Matthew, or of John . . . . These matters are of real importance, but to begin with them would improperly divert us from our primary concern.

The issue which has been posed for us by the history of Christian thought on the matter is whether we should or should not see Jesus as a political figure. There are numerous reasons for arguing that we should not:

a. Jesus came into a society where many believed themselves to be near the end of history. He seems to have shared the understanding that the coming kingdom of God would put an end to ordinary historical process. It then made no sense to care about creating or maintaining institutions, or any of the rest of the concern for ordinary political life. If the expectation of the impending historical end has any meaning, it is that political process matters less.

b. Jesus was intentionally personalistic. He reduced all relationships to matters of face-to-face openness and love. Ethical questions of a structural character do not come into view from that perspective.

c. The purpose of Jesus was to give his life as an atonement for sins. The meaning of his death is therefore ritual or soteriological. It would be misunderstood if we were to speak of anything about his public life leading up to that event as representing political or even ethical decisions.

d. There is the docetic understanding of Jesus as not really making human decisions because of his unique metaphysical dignity as Son of God.

In these and other ways, most of the Christian tradition has given us a picture of a depoliticized Jesus. For some few people (like Tolstoy or some monks or mystics), it follows that we should be depoliticized in turn. On the other hand, for most Christians it means that in our political activity we should not be guided by the teachings or the example of Jesus.

It was appropriate to ask first this general and formal question—"Is Jesus political?"—in order to sharpen our sensitivity as we read the gospel accounts. I now propose only to look at very well-known texts, adding nothing original to the reading of them by way of erudition but only the light that falls on them when we ask straightforwardly, "Is there political meaning here?"

Our first document indicating with some fullness who Jesus was expected to be is the annunciation:

> You must name him "YHWH liberates"
> He will be great and will be called the Son
> of the most high
> the Lord God will give him the throne of his
> ancestor David.[1]

The response of Mary to this information is the text we call the *magnificat*, which describes a social and economic reversal:

> He has shown the power of his arm
> He has routed the proud of heart
> He has pulled down princes from their thrones
>   and exalted the lowly
> the hungry he has filled with good things
>   the rich sent empty away."[2]

Another powerful testimony to the expectation Jesus came to meet is found in the words of John, who, when asked by his listeners what it would mean to "bear fruit worthy of repentance," responded,

---

[1] Luke 1:31-32—"And now, you will conceive in your womb and bear a son, and you will name him Jesus. He will be great, and will be called the Son of the Most High, and the Lord God will give to him the throne of his ancestor David."

[2] Luke 1:51-53—"He has shown strength with his arm; he has scattered the proud in the thoughts of their hearts. He has brought down the powerful from their thrones, and lifted up the lowly; he has filled the hungry with good things, and sent the rich away empty."

> whoever has two tunics shall share with the
>> one who has none
> the one with something to eat must do the same.[3]

Specifically, two categories of listeners are named who were not satisfied with that answer. Those listeners are identified in political terms. They were the tax gatherers, the instruments of the financing of the Roman presence, and the soldiers who enforced that presence. John directs instructions to both of them, radically limiting the use they could make of their power.

If we were to add the expectations of the magi from the East in Matthew's Gospel, or the promise of the angels who spoke to the shepherds, or the fear of Herod, the picture would only be more fully the same: Jesus came to a Jewish people awaiting a liberator, and he never told them he was not the one they were waiting for.

We take our next question—"Was Jesus apolitical?"—to the temptation accounts in Matthew and Luke. Jesus faced ways to go about being the "Son of God" whom his baptism has designated him to be. "Son of God," as in the Psalms, means not a divine/human being but the king. The opportunities presented to Jesus by the tempter in the desert are all ways of being the king: seizing royal authority or moving the people to acclaim him as their ruler. Let the temptation to make bread suffice as an example. We know from the later report that when Jesus fed a multitude in the desert with miraculous bread, they wanted to make him king. Jesus' ministry is therefore initiated with a dramatic symbolic testing of what Jesus is willing to do in order to be king. Had his intention been authentically apolitical, the temptations would not have been temptations.

The story continues with the programmatic statement made by Jesus in the synagogue at Nazareth when he was given to read the scroll of Isaiah opened at chapter 61. He announced to the gathering there that in his presence the promise of liberation and the promulgation of a Year of Jubilee was fulfilled. That descrip-

---

[3] Luke 3:11—"In reply he said to them: 'Whoever has two coats must share with anyone who has none; and whoever has food must do likewise.'"

tion of a new order which his presence brought into history was then further explicated in the blessings and woes of chapter 6, where we are told that the coming of the kingdom will be bad for the rich and good for the poor, good for those who mourn and bad for those who now rejoice, because the last will be first and the first last. As in Matthew's version of the Sermon on the Mount, the culmination of the newness which the kingdom brings is love not only for the friend but for the enemy, because therein one sees the nature of the Father who "himself is kind to the ungrateful and the wicked" (Luke 6:35).

In the middle of his ministry, Jesus warns his listeners that to follow him will be costly. In John 6, a division within his movement begins after the feeding of the multitude in response to his "hard words" about sharing his suffering. In Luke's Gospel, we find that "great crowds were following" Jesus (14:25). He warned them that truly following him would mean willingness to risk everything, including the most elemental social solidarity of the family. He warned people against deciding too lightly to join his movement for fear of later shame and failure.

He said—before his own crucifixion—that "bearing the cross" would be the cost of discipleship: the cross was the way Romans treated people who threatened the civil peace. In the account of the passion, just after the first "Lord's Supper," we find that Jesus' disciples were arguing among themselves as to which would have the positions of authority in the coming kingdom. His response is at the same time his explanation of his own choice:

> Among the pagans it is the kings who lord it over them
> those who have authority over them are given the title
> "benefactor"
> it must not happen with you . . .
> Here I am among you as one who serves.[4]

---

[4] Luke 22:25-27—"But he said to them: 'The kings of the Gentiles lord it over them; and those in authority over them are called benefactors. But not so with you; rather the greatest among you must become like the youngest, and the leader like one who serves. For who is greater, the one who is at the table or the one who serves? Is it not the one at the table? But I am among you as one who serves.'"

Even then, Jesus knew it was the temptation of his closest follow-
ers to conceive of the coming kingdom as a matter of civil sovereignty exercised by virtue of righteous violence. He knew they
were tempted, because that had been his temptation.

The temptation is repeated once more in the garden a few
minutes later. The aura of reverence surrounding the passion
story often keeps us from asking concretely what the temptation
was in those last hours. Yet if we do ask, the answer is unavoidable: Jesus was still tempted to take the path of the Zealots, to use
righteous revolutionary violence to drive the Romans from his
country and renew the possibility for God's people to live according to God's law. That was Jesus' temptation. He was not tempted
to be a cenobite in the deserts of Judea, nor to be a Sadducee in
Jerusalem; he was tempted to lead a righteous revolution against
the pagan empire.

When Jesus rejected that temptation, it was not in favor of
doing nothing, nor in favor of social withdrawal, nor was it a
concern with ritual alone or even with mystical contemplation
or gnostic information. His alternative was the gathering of a
new kind of people. He did not establish a guerrilla unit to bring
down the Romans, nor a house of contemplation, nor a theological faculty, but a people: a structured community best described
by the name "assembly" (ecclesia). That name normally designated
a town meeting or a parliament qualified to do business on behalf
of a city. The body Jesus gathered was constituted in new ways,
by voluntary decision rather than by geography or biology. It had
new decision-making patterns, by dialogue and consensus rather
than authority. It had new ways of dealing with the offender, by
forgiveness instead of vengeance. It had new ways of dealing with
social stratification, by honoring the woman, the slave, the child,
and the outsider. It had new ways of dealing with money, by sharing it. Let it be noted that all of these marks of the originality of
the community we call "church" are social and political. They
have to do with money, power, status, and making decisions.

The interpretation of the import of the career of Jesus as
nonviolent liberator for today easily breaks down into two different debates. One set of Christians cannot conceive that Jesus was

tempted to be a Zealot. To them, we must say that they misunder-
stand the whole meaning of his work if they do not see the passion and zeal with which he saw himself to be called to proclaim
the breaking in of God's sovereignty in matters of human justice
and the beginning of a new order among men and women. If we
are not tempted by the Zealot option as he was, then our renunciation of the Zealot means of revolutionary violence cannot mean
what it meant for him. If we are passive, or quietist, or tired, or
patient with the fallenness and oppressiveness of the world, we
fail to see in him authentically the anointed one, the one who was
to bring down the mighty from their thrones and exalt the lowly.

On the other side, there are those who do share the passion
for liberation but who believe, with the Zealots, that the means
of that change can appropriately be righteous violence. In so
reasoning, they incorporate the pragmatism of modern social
understanding according to which it is possible with simple
augmentation of coercive power to bring about whatever social
results one wishes, regardless of the rights or dignities of those
who stand in the way. They see the righteousness of their cause as
authorizing them to deal with their adversaries in a way opposite
to that of Jesus for the sake of the goals which they would claim
to be those of Jesus.

We shall best understand the novelty of Jesus' new answer,
which was neither quietism nor Zealotry, if we recognize how it
cuts across the grain of recent patterns of social ethical analysis.
What all of these patterns have in common is that they relegate
our response to Jesus' call to love the enemy to some other
plane of reality than the real world. The recent patterns can be
described as follows.

1. *Recent theological tradition has told us that we must choose
between the Jesus of history and the Jesus of dogma.*

If Jesus is the divine Word incarnate, then what we will
be concerned about is the metaphysical transactions by means
of which he saved humanity by entering into it. We will then
leap, like the creed, from the birth of Jesus to the cross. His
teachings and his social and political involvement will be of little
interest and not binding for us.

If, on the other hand, we seek to understand the "Jesus of history" in his human context, as it is reconstructed by the historical
disciplines, this will be in order to find a man like any other, a
reforming rabbi fully within the limits attainable by our human
explanations and who is sometimes mistaken, especially about
the future, and whose authority over us will depend on what we
ourselves can consent to grant to his teachings.

The nineteenth century chose the Jesus of history until
Albert Schweitzer showed us that Jesus "as he really was" really
did take himself to be an apocalyptic figure and his age to be
the one just before the new order begins.[5] Then the systematic
tradition veered back to metaphysics, using literary criticism to
demonstrate how the gospel documents project that existential
self-awareness of the young church onto Jesus—an awareness so
closely tied to the name of Jesus, but not to his historical reality,
that if he had not really been who he was, it would not jeopardize
anything of his "meaning" for us.

If we confess Jesus as Messiah, we must refuse this choice.
The Jesus of history is the Christ of faith. It is in hearing the revolutionary rabbi that we understand the existential freedom which
is asked of the church. As we look closer at the Jesus whom Albert
Schweitzer rediscovered, in all his eschatological realism, we find
an utterly precise and practicable ethical instruction, practicable
because in him the kingdom has actually come within reach. The
sovereignty of YHWH has become human history in him.

2. *The tradition tells us that we are obligated to choose between the
prophet and the institution.*

The prophet condemns and crushes us under his demand for
perfection. He is right, ultimately, both in convincing us of our
sinfulness and in pointing us toward the ideal which, although
unattainable, must remain our goal. But as far as that social
order is concerned, which is up to us to administer today and
tomorrow, his demands are without immediate relevance. Love,

---

[5] Yoder is referring to Albert Schweitzer's landmark survey of various historical approaches to Jesus that also presents his own significant conclusions.
See Schweitzer, *The Quest of the Historical Jesus* (Minneapolis: Augsburg Fortress,
2001).

self-sacrifice, and nonviolence provide no basis for taking responsibility in this world. Dependent upon the grace of God alone, one cannot act in history. Those who are called to assure the survival and the administration of institutions will therefore accept violence in order to diminish or eliminate it one day. They will accept inequality and exploitation with the goal of progressively combating them. This is a very modest task, and one gets one's hands dirty, but it is an indispensable task if something worse is to be prevented. While respecting the prophet, the rest of us will choose the institution.

The new regime instituted by Jesus as Messiah forbids us to make this choice. The Jubilee and kingdom which Jesus proclaims are not the end of time, pure event without duration, unconnected to either yesterday or tomorrow. The Jubilee is precisely an *institution* whose functioning within history will have a precise, practicable, limited impact. The kingdom is an order. It is not a perpetual social earthquake rendering impossible any continuity of temporal effort but a periodic revision permitting new beginnings.

3. *The tradition tells us to choose between the catastrophic kingdom and the inner kingdom.*

Jesus announced the imminent certain end of history as an event which could happen tomorrow or which was, at the latest, sure to come soon after his death. The apostles maintained this intensity of expectation for a few decades, but finally it had to be admitted that there had been a mistake about the date, or perhaps about what they were looking for so soon.

The other option begins by assuming that Jesus could not have been wrong. It must then be concluded that he was speaking of the kingdom of God and its coming only in order to teach, by means of the mythical language which was current in his time, about an inner, spiritual, existential kingdom whose reality will always remain properly hidden to the eyes of the unbelievers and of the historian.

Once again, if Jesus is the Christ, we must refuse this choice. The kingdom of God is a social order and not a hidden one. It is not a universal catastrophe independent of the will of men; it is that concrete jubilary obedience (in pardon and repentance), the possibility of which is proclaimed beginning right now, opening up the real accessibility of a new order in which grace and justice are linked that men have only to accept. It does not assume time will end tomorrow; it reveals why it is meaningful that history should go on at all.

Jesus had also predicted that men would refuse this offer and promise, pushing away the kingdom that had come close to them. He was not mistaken.

4. *The tradition tells us we must choose between the political and the sectarian.*

In the tradition of Ernst Troeltsch, Western theological ethics assumes that the choice of options is fixed in logic and fixed for all times and places by the way the Constantinian heritage dealt with the question.[6] Either one accepts the responsibility of politics without serious qualification (i.e., the duty of governing), with whatever means that takes, or one chooses a withdrawn position of either personal-monastic-vocational or sectarian character, which is "apolitical." If you choose to share fully in the duties and the guilt of the government, you are exercising responsibility and are politically relevant; if you choose not to, it is because you think politics is either unimportant or impure and are more concerned for other matters, such as your own salvation. In so doing, you would have Jesus on your side, but having Jesus on your side is not enough, for there are issues to which Jesus does not speak. (Here this view overlaps with and appeals to the other three already sketched.) Therefore, we must supplement and in effect correct what we learn from him, by adding information on the nature and the goodness of the specifically "political" which we gain from other sources.

If Jesus is confessed as Messiah, this disjunction is illegitimate. To say that any position is "apolitical" is to deny the powerful (sometimes conservative, sometimes revolutionary) impact

---

[6] Ernst Troeltsch's (1865–1923) monumental two-volume *The Social Teaching of the Christian Churches*, trans. Olive Wyon (Louisville, Ky.: Westminster John Knox, 1992), stands behind the position Yoder criticizes here.

on society made by the creation of an alternative social group, and to overrate both the power and the manageability of those particular social structures identified as "political." To assume that "being politically relevant" is itself a univocal option, so that in saying "yes" to it one knows where one is going, is to overestimate the capacity of "the nature of politics" to dictate its own direction.

Because Jesus' particular way of rejecting the sword and at the same time condemning those who wielded it *was* politically relevant, both the Sanhedrin and the procurator had to deny him the right to live in the name of both of their forms of political responsibility. His alternative was so relevant, so much a threat, that Pilate could afford to free, in exchange for Jesus, the ordinary Guevara-type insurrectionist Barabbas. Jesus' way is not less but more relevant to the question of how society moves than is the struggle for possession of the levers of command. Pilate and Caiaphas testify to this by their judgment on him.

One can sympathize with those who think that problems of substance can be swept away by semantic conventions. Some would say that there is such a difference of character between Jesus and what the whole world considers as politically relevant that we should grant the definition of the "political" as best represented by what Jesus rejects. Then Jesus would be "apolitical" after all, taking for himself and his disciples a withdrawn stance. After thus agreeing on definitions, we could then go on to argue the moral justification, and perhaps also the political relevance on some other level, of the apolitical stance, but at least we would not need to stumble over diversities of definition. Jesus chose not only to stumble over diversities of definition but to be crucified on them. He refused to concede that the men in power represent an ideal definition, a logically proper definition, or even an empirically acceptable definition of what it means to be political. He did not say (as some sectarian pacifists, or some pietists might), "You can have your politics, and I shall do something else more important"; he said, "Your definition of *polis*, of the social, of the wholeness of man in his socialness, is perverted."

5. *The tradition tells us we must choose between the individual and the social.*

The "ethics of the Sermon on the Mount" is for face-to-face personal encounters; an ethic of the "secular vocation" is needed for social structures. Faith will restore the individual's soul, and Jesus' strong language about love for neighbor will help with this. But then how a restored man should act will be decided on grounds to which the radical personalism of Jesus does not speak.

But Jesus does not know anything about radical personalism. The personhood which he proclaims as a healing, forgiving call to all is integrated into the social novelty of the healing community. This is clear from the Lukan text we have read; it would be even more clear if we could read the Jesus story with a stronger sense of the Jewishness of his context and with Amos ringing in our ears. The more we learn about the Jewishness of Jesus (from archaeology and from new textual finds, as well as from growing respect for rabbinical studies on the part of Christian theologians), the more evident it becomes that he could not have been perceived by his contemporaries otherwise than as we have portrayed him here. In fact, to be fully honest, we must turn the point around: the idea of Jesus as an individualist or a teacher of radical personalism could arise only in the (Protestant, post-pietist, rationalist) context where it did (i.e., in a context which, if not intentionally anti-Semitic, was at least sweepingly a-Semitic, a stranger to the Jewish Jesus).

We could extend the list of traditional antinomies of which we must repent if we are to understand Jesus. Tradition tells us to choose between respect for persons and participation in the movement of history; Jesus refuses, because the movement of history is personal. There is no choosing between spirit and flesh, between theory and praxis, between belief and behavior, between the ideal and the possible.

Chapter 8

Early Christian Cosmology and Nonviolence

What we mean here by "cosmology" is not a systematic effort to describe in general the way the first Christians thought about the shape of the world but, rather, an attempt to identify specific points at which we can see how their thought was different from ours, and how this can help us to make sense of their witness and way in the world.

In a previous lecture, I already identified one such point. I argued that believing Jews, listening to Jesus against the background of their memories of the repeated miraculous savings of Israel reported in their Scriptures, would have been able to understand the message of Jesus about a coming kingdom without erecting between Jesus and themselves the barrier of a worldview assuming that no saving wonders can ever happen.

Now we turn to the apostolic literature with the same kind of question. I suggest that we select one specific body of images which we find widely scattered and never formally explained in the writings of Paul. In only eight or ten passages, but in a recognizable way, Paul writes about "principalities and powers, thrones and dominions. . . ." The lists of names of mysterious entities are different each time but recognizably refer to the same background. There are realities, which we shall henceforth most simply refer to as *exousiae*, or "powers," which have something to do with our historical experience. These passages have constituted a puzzle to Christian observers who have for centuries avoided reading them carefully. One set of interpreters, meaning to be conservative and to believe whatever the text says, neverthe-less did not work hard at understanding what it does say. Some of these identified the *exousiae* with the demons which "possessed" people and which Jesus expelled, but this connection is not sup-ported by anything in the text. Others assume that the reference is to personal archangels in the style of Michael or of Gabriel, anthropomorphic persons with particular tasks under God in the guidance of history. But the Pauline language (although some-times we find *angeloi* within the list) does not indicate any interest in describing the personalities or the individual identities of any of these *exousiae*.

More recent scholars have assumed that we have in these texts leftovers of some kind of mythic or magical worldview, positing the existence of intelligences within the created world, and have assumed that the enlightened thing to do with the texts is to ignore them and to forgive the apostolic generation for not hav-ing completely overcome its mythological worldview.

Thus one set of readers intended to believe what the Bible said but have made no sense of it, and another set have assumed that they knew what it meant but they need not believe it.

A new seriousness in facing these texts was represented when the Reformed theologian Hendrik Berkhof,[1] during the Nazi occupation of the Netherlands, began a more creative and trust-ing synthesis of the Pauline texts on the powers. The synthesis he developed in a simple series of expositions, first published in 1952, was in no way original or contrary to what critical scholar-ship could see in those texts. But he reached past the embarrass-ment of liberal and conservative exegetes to lift from those texts something like a philosophy of history or a historicist cosmology. Although we see it only in brief allusions, like the separate out-croppings of a stratum of rock which the geologists teach us to discern as part of the same rock even though it shows at different places on the surface of the soil, it represents a coherent view of history and of the cosmic struggle in our own age.

---

[1] The text to which Yoder refers is *Christ and the Powers* (Scottdale, Pa.: Herald, 1962).

The *exousiae*, first of all, are creatures of God. They did not come into being on their own or out of nothing (they are less profound in either description or prescription), but they received their being from the created purposes of a God who willed to have an order. The powers do not exist from all eternity, nor do they bring themselves into being or arise out of nothing; they are creatures of God, made with a purpose, and part of the cosmos intended to exist for God's glory.

The purpose for which the powers are created is the service of God and mankind. They are to make life possible by providing an order within which life can have meaning. The powers have, however, rebelled against God and refused to discharge their function of service to human life. Instead, they have become autonomous, they have made absolute claims for their authority over us, and they have thereby become our lords rather than our servants.

Since, however, God's creative grace is not revocable, the powers do not go out of existence when they have ceased to be obedient; they do continue to be able to rule over us. Thus the lostness of the fallen human condition is not simply that every individual is or becomes personally a sinner. It is also that the structures which surround us have become instruments of our subjugation, not of our empowerment.

In his crucifixion, Christ is the victim of the powers. They put him to death. His death is not an accident, nor the deed of specific evil individuals, but the product of the consistent out-working of the nature of things in the fallen cosmos operating according to their own character.

At the same time, Jesus is victor over the powers. Their effort to save their sovereignty from challenge by destroying his life is frustrated by the willingness of his death and the power of his resurrection.

The text from the Hebrew Scriptures which is most frequently cited in the New Testament is not a reference to the law of love for God and neighbor, nor to sacrifice for sins, but to the divine oracle of Psalm 110:

The Lord said to my Lord,
"Sit at my right hand
until I make your enemies your footstool."[2]

The early Christians understood themselves to be beginning to live in a new age in which Christ, seated at the right hand of the Father, was waging a war against defeated forces of the fallen world, defeated in principle yet unruly. In the language of Colossians, these forces had been "disarmed" and "made a public spectacle."[3] To say that Christ is Lord does not mean only a declaration of personal allegiance but a statement about the shape and destiny of the cosmos. He must reign until all his enemies are under his feet (1 Cor 15:25): that is the significance of present history. Ultimately, every tongue will confess that Jesus Christ is Lord (Phil 2:11). That includes the supra- and infraterrestrial powers against which we are currently doing battle (Eph 6:12).

In all of this description of how Paul thinks about the powers, I have proceeded, as does Paul, without specifying what kinds of entities he is talking about. Some Christians have attempted to telescope this set of concepts with that of demon possession, but the field of meanings is quite different. There is no indication that exorcism is their destiny. Others have attempted to relate them to the world of angels understood as ministering spirits. But we know very little about what biblical writers thought about angels, and much of what is said about the *exousiae* uses quite different vocabulary and does not give much reason for ascribing anthropomorphic personality to them.

The best modern rendering is probably our very flexible concept of "structure." In our European usage, "structure" may mean the work of an architect, or a pattern of social interaction, or a pattern of psychological response. It may designate law or custom. At many points in our experience, a whole is more than the sum of its parts: things and events have meaning not only atomistically

---

[2] Psalm 110:1—"The LORD says to my lord, 'Sit at my right hand until I make your enemies your footstool.'"

[3] Colossians 2:15—"He disarmed the rulers and authorities and made a public example of them, triumphing over them in it."

but as part of a context which exists before and beyond them, though it would not exist without them. To be human is to exist within a network of structures (physical, social, linguistic, historical . . .); to be fallen humans is to exist within a fallen network of fallen structures. This way of describing the human predicament seems to be a far more adequate way to describe the complexity of creaturely existence in a fallen history than some of the other classical understandings like "the orders of creation," natural law, or "realism."

This simple outline of the Pauline perspective has been persuasive. It "fits" and has been widely borrowed. Permit an example whose appropriateness is precisely that it is not rare but representative: three years ago, the Division of World Mission and Evangelism of the World Council of Churches convened a world conference in Melbourne, Australia, under the title "Your Kingdom Come." What does it mean for the Christian community to live and pray that petition? The inaugural address, presented by the moderator of the Commission on World Mission and Evangelism, Dr. Soritua A. E. Nababan, reached naturally for this Pauline language:

> In public life, to pray "Your Kingdom Come" is to ask the full revelation of what Christ did: "He disarmed the principalities and powers and made a public example of them, triumphing over them in him" (Col. 2:15). It is to ask and therefore to work for the end of the powers which are the ordered structures of society and the spiritual powers which lie behind them and undergird religious structures, intellectual structures, moral structures, political structures—the religious undergirdings of stable ancient and primitive saints, all the "ologies" and the "isms," all the codes and customs, all the tyranny of the market, the school, the courts, race, and nation.[4]

---

[4] See Soritua Nababan, *Your Kingdom Come: Mission Perspectives, Report on the World Conference on Mission and Evangelism* (Geneva: World Council of Churches, 1980), 3. Nababan was also the general secretary of the Council of Churches, Indonesia.

From the perspective of the rediscovery of this more adequate Pauline cosmology, it is clear that one can no longer say, as conservative religious groups would, that the gospel deals only with personal ethics and not with social structures. The *exousiae* cannot be *identified* with social structures but are most adequately understood as a larger reality, of which visible oppressive structures are the manifestation. The cross deals with them as much as it does with personal guilt or personal destiny. The New Testament does not say that the only way to change structures is to change the heart of an individual person (preferably the person in power so that that person will use his authority for good).

On the other hand, Paul does not identify the coming of the kingdom either in the provisional form already achieved by Christ or in the ultimate form to which we now look forward as brought about by the simple seizure of the controls of the present fallen social system, as if all that is wrong with the system were the fact that the wrong people are governing it. The liberation which has begun already is not that the *exousiae*, as they are, will be used for good by good people instead of being used for evil by evil people. Their continuing rebelliousness will be transformed at those points where believers, like their Lord, will refuse the idolatrous pretentions of the *exousiae*. The passage from Ephesians (3:10) says it the most simply. The existence of the new humanity of Jew and Gentile sharing their bread in one body announces to the powers their loss of sovereignty.

Thus we have a social vision which is both pessimistic and optimistic. It is both more critical and more hopeful than those which seek to be guided by a vision of the order of creation or of nature. It sees the cross as power and not weakness. It sees the love of enemy as liberation and not subjugation. When am I more a slave of my adversary than when I let him define our relationship as my being his enemy? The simplest meaning of the incarnation is that God in Jesus refused to let us define him as our enemy. Thus it was that the early Christians saw their counterculture lifestyle without power not as a deprivation but as the beginning of the new world. They did not renounce bloodshed as an instrument of the kingdom because there were less costly ways to proceed, but because it is incompatible with the nature of the coming kingdom.

A second point at which it will do us good to struggle with the distance between the apostolic worldview and our own is that stance, or that kind of literature, which we characterize as "apocalyptic." The term has many meanings. What is of interest to us just now is the fact that it describes a view of the historical process which does not see the way things go as being under human control. What matters in understanding "apocalyptic" is not the difficulty of imagery like the sky rolling up in the form of a scroll or the stars falling to earth. Rather, it is a vision of the historical process in which the believer does not assume any access to or control of how things go. The believer does not claim to understand social systems and their development or to be in such a position as to influence them.

Since the Age of Enlightenment, Western humanism claims that we both understand the world system and are in charge of it. The debates which divide our culture are between differing views of how that understanding should be expressed and which of us should control the events. Yet the effects of our seeing the world this way have not been encouraging. The points at which we have felt most sovereign over creation (such as in the exploitation of natural resources) and the points at which we have felt most qualified to be sovereign over our neighbors (such as in the dominant Christian cultures of slavery, empire, and military diplomacy) have been the points in which history has most evidently "gotten out of hand."

Most Christian thinkers have not yet adjusted to the collapse of the vision of human sufficiency and control. Yet that adjustment is beginning. We are beginning to adjust to the recognition that the sense in which Europe was "Christian" for a millennium and a half was deceptive and confusing. Whether it be in western Europe with the declining significance of institutional Christianity in the face of postreligious secularism; or in eastern Europe in societies administered in line with a specific atheist ideology; or in Latin America, where centuries of traditional Christian administration have only set the scene for differing forms of tyranny; or in the rest of the globe, where Christians never were in control, adjustments are beginning which accept—sometimes grudgingly and sometimes wholeheartedly—that the church in our age (like Judaism since Jeremiah) is called first of all to diaspora faithfulness. When, in times of particular grace, it is given to believers to contribute effectively to the shaping of their society, this will never be rejected, but the assumption that that must always be the case can now be set aside as a deceptive dream. Therefore, the assumption that we need an ethical system to adjust to our sharing in the seizure of power—a theology of just wars, of just revolutions, and of righteous empire—can be set aside as our form of the temptation which Jesus rejected in the desert and again in the garden.

John, on the island of Patmos, wept because no one was able to unseal the scroll which he saw in the hand of the one seated on the throne.[5] To translate, no one could explain the meaning of the history in which John and his fellow believers found themselves, still oppressed three generations after Pentecost. Then he saw on the scene a figure who had not been there before: the "Lamb" bearing the signs of his having been slain. Then he heard the heavenly creatures and the whole universe break into "a new song," a song which could not have been sung before, rejoicing that the Lamb was "worthy to receive power, because by his blood he was purchasing for God people of every tribe and tongue and nation."[6] To translate, the meaning of history is the reconciling work of the church. The meaning of history is not carried by Caesars and Cromwells, military liberators ancient or modern, as much as by the creation of a new human fellowship through the cross, defined precisely by transcending enmity between classes of people. This does not make our efforts to understand the fallen world systematically and to contribute as we can to relative justice and liberation unimportant. This does not render our refusal to

[5] Revelation 5:4—"And I began to weep bitterly because no one was found worthy to open the scroll or look into it."

[6] Revelation 5:9—"They sing a new song: 'You are worthy to take the scroll and to open its seals, for you were slaughtered and by your blood you ransomed for God saints from every tribe and language and people and nation.'"

collaborate in unjust systems and our conscientious and costly participation in relatively more just systems, despite their imperfection, unimportant. It does deny to us either a need or a right to so glorify our passing human systems that we would arrogate to ourselves the authority to destroy our fellow human beings in the name of any such cause.

As we began, in an earlier lecture, to interpret the political meaning of the ministry of Jesus, we noted that many modern readers claim to know *a priori* that we have little to learn from him because his world is so far from ours. Further, many recent interpreters of later apostolic thought (i.e., that of Paul) assume the superiority of our grasp of the direction of cosmic process. This has applied especially to the two aspects of the early Christian cosmology we have just looked at: its vision of the powers and its apocalyptic hope. In no segment of contemporary moral thought has that detachment from the New Testament vision been more weighty or more powerful in producing a change in moral understanding than with regard to the moral legitimacy of violence.

If it should be the case that Jesus is more politically relevant than had long been thought (as I argued in the other lecture)[7] or that the apostolic vision of the historical process is more realistic than was thought, then that will not be merely a corrective on the formal level concerning how seriously to take certain ancient texts. It also becomes a new perspective on the appropriateness of the nonviolent morality which we had been told was outmoded. Thus the more empathetic vision of the Scriptures as our still-living canon has more to tell us than the "realism" which claims to be describing the only choices permitted by the world around us but which, in truth, has less to say about fallenness and hope than the apostles.

---

[7] See chapter 7, pp. 85-96.

Chapter 9

Varieties of Catholic Peace Theology I
Nonviolent Spirituality

The image of Catholic culture which seems self-evident in a nation dominated by a millennium or more of the presence of one church, as in Italy or Ireland or Poland, stands in strong contrast to the American scene. If speaking of an ancient Catholic culture, one would not choose "diversity" as a characteristic both desirable and in need of explanation.

Although a few Christians of Catholic conviction were present in the American colonies from the beginning, they were numerically insignificant. Only the nineteenth century brought Catholics in large numbers to build the cities and the factories of a nation eager to catch up with the models of industrialization projected by the western European nations. By the end of that century, Catholicism had still made no impact on the dominantly Protestant public consciousness of the nation, although there were cities in which neighborhood political power was in the hands of Catholic majorities. It was not until 1928 that a Roman Catholic could be thought of as a candidate for the office of President,[1] but many believed he could not be elected primarily because of his confession. Only in 1960 was it possible for a Catholic to be elected as President. Even he, John F. Kennedy, had to take pains in the course of his campaign to assure the

---

[1] Yoder is referring to Al Smith, the Democratic presidential candidate from New York who lost to Herbert Hoover in the 1928 presidential election.

voters that his religious commitment would never interfere with his political duties.

It is thus constitutive of the Roman Catholic presence in North America that it has come to terms with being an outvoted minority in national life. Sometimes this has led to extreme forms of patriotic accommodation in order to attempt to assure Protestants that Catholics were good Americans. Other times it has meant a posture of defensive separation, as in the great investment made in creating a network of alternate schools.

A second kind of diversity also created new challenges for pastors and theologians in America. Sizable populations came to the United States from Ireland, from Italy, from Poland and Slovakia, and from Bavaria. For each of them, Catholic identity had historically meant ethnic unity; now they find themselves in the same diocese with each other. Their theology says that they are all members of one church, and they accept the authority of one bishop, but seldom can a local parish prosper without limiting itself to one ethnic identity. In recent decades, the influx of Spanish-speaking Catholics from the southwestern states and from Central America has been added to this mixture as well. That the Catholic Church is a worldwide unity had for a long time been a statement of faith; only in America did people find themselves obligated to experience that unity within just one city. As modern liturgical renewal moved away from the monopoly of Latin, the diversity became even greater, since some of these communities, especially those of Spanish language, moved toward a vernacular worship in their ancestral tongue and others moved to English.

Thus, even in its internal self-understanding, American Catholicism had begun, well before the middle of this century, to outgrow the commonsense assumption of identity between the church and the nation which has been so self-evident in Europe.

A third source of unprecedented diversity arose from the interaction of the first two. Becoming integrated in America did not happen in one way but in many places and, therefore, in many ways. There was no central American office to orchestrate the process of adaptation. Facing social issues for which earlier tradition did not equip them, seeking to be guided by papal directives prepared for a different world just beginning to change, carried along like any minority group by different rates of adaptation in different generations, yet pressed more than many adapting minorities by the authority claims of the magisterium and ethnic consensus, American Catholicism experienced a fermentation and fragmentation which tended to reproduce the pluralism of the rest of America, although with some time lag.

It should, therefore, be no surprise that the persons and movements of whom I am preparing to speak will not stand side by side simply as more than one example of the same phenomenon. They will manifest genuine diversity of style and conception. What I am to describe may be spoken of as a "movement" in the broad sense it has come to have, namely, a discernable commonality of numerous initiatives not coordinated from one center or dictated by one doctrine but which can be seen to be moving along one path.

The way in which Roman Catholics in the United States think about themselves has been strongly influenced by the way in which they have become aware of their differences from Protestants and from postreligious members of a pluralistic society. This focus upon the distinctiveness of Catholicism as a denomination has created a self-understanding very different from what it meant to be Catholic in a nearly monolithic European homeland—in Ireland or Italy or Poland—from which the grandparents of these North American Catholics had come. This shift of awareness results in a misunderstanding and an unintentional changing of balance which has been thought about very little.

Because Catholics differ from Protestants about the status of natural law, as this is debated within the academic profession of moral theology, it has come to be thought that that notion of "nature" is central within Catholic experience and piety as well. Because Catholics differ with Protestants about the place of the episcopal magisterium, American Catholics have tended to assume a special concern for arguing about the particular points at which bishops had expressed themselves.

Because Catholics and Protestants differ about the sacrament of penance, American Catholics have felt a duty to care especially about canon law, the limits it sets, and the way it changes from one codification to the next.

A very important corrective has recently been brought into American Catholic life at these points. It is very possibly not a matter which needs to be talked about in Poland, but it needs to be rediscovered in America.

The heart of the moral life of the ordinary Catholic believer is neither in canon law nor in episcopal loyalty nor in natural law. It has more to do with the lives of the saints, with the cultivation of virtues, and with the lived experience of family and community. On all of these levels, there has recently been a new working of the Holy Spirit within American Catholic culture, and much of it has had to do with peace and nonviolence.

Before moving on to the narrative about persons, let us note some of the other powerful components of Catholic moral culture. One element of Catholic theological identity has always been the notion of *absolute law*. The law of God is revealed in such a way that it can be known without our always knowing why it is that way, just as the decree of a human sovereign can be held to be binding simply because it has been edicted independently of the extent to which his subjects agree with it, understand the reasons behind it, or trust its hoped-for wholesome social effects.

So it is that if God is a revealer whose word makes known his will, it will not always be up to our insight or agreement to ratify the bindingness of what he says. His law, therefore, need not make sense in our perspective or cohere logically with a theory of social analysis or mechanism of social action. If God is God, especially if we are ignorant and sinful, there must be times when we must simply let ourselves be told, "That is his will. Do it!"

This sense of the simple authority of revelation is more at home in the Franciscan tradition than in the Dominican or Jesuit schools. It is a minority position within Catholic thought, but, nonetheless, one which has historical and logical claims. It has never been declared heretical, and it is deeply rooted in piety.

The Austrian theologian Johannes Ude was the strongest advocate of this view among professional theologians in this period. He entitled his book *Thou Shall Not Kill.*[2] The very concept of a revealed divine command is, by its nature, not subject to calculation or negotiation. The sacredness of life is not something that can be relativized or bargained against some other value. Something of this simplicity was probably also within the background of the uneducated Austrian conscientious objector Franz Jägerstätter, although his explanation of his position drew on other sources as well.[3]

Another classical pattern of moral reasoning in Roman Catholicism has always been *the cultivation of virtue.* This is a very different focus of attention from the absolute law of God, yet it has in common with that approach a relative unconcern for pragmatic measurement of the situation. A Christian, by nature, is meek, or is ready to suffer, or is a servant, or is nonviolent. The true Christian is one for whom the cultivation of that character is a dominant commitment which effectively determines her or his way of living and being.

It is obvious that this concentration upon the Christian life as a matter of quality rather than impact is most at home within the disciplined religious life. That makes it easy for Protestants to disqualify it as not involved with the real world, or as self-righteous. Nonetheless, this heritage of religious discipline has made it possible, through the centuries, for some Catholics—despite the dominance of the just war tradition—to have kept their minds and their elbows free to have room for the continued confession of the contemplation of the full meaning of Jesus as not only savior figure, but model.

---

[2] Johannes Ude (1874–1965) was arrested and sentenced to death during World War II. The collapse of the Nazi occupation occurred before his sentence was carried out, and after the war he frequently wrote about pacifism. The text to which Yoder refers specifically is *Du Sollst Nicht Töten* (Dornbirn: Mayer, 1948).

[3] Franz Jägerstätter (1907–1943) was another Austrian who refused to comply with the demands of Nazi occupation during World War II. For his conscientious objection, he was beheaded on August 9, 1943. On October 26, 2007, Jägerstätter was beatified by the Roman Catholic Church.

It is by no means the case that this priority commitment to the nature of virtue must lead to social inefficacy. It involves its own style of historical impact. No one cay say that Saint Francis, or Dorothy Day, or Mother Teresa of Calcutta have been without social impact. Their pattern for decision making and goal setting is one which bypasses the social-mechanism models of cultural process which Western intellectuals have come to trust. In the religious community where ritual and spirituality are assumed to be as real as mechanism, this should not all be considered a disadvantage. Thus it has been natural, and should have been no surprise, that one of the foundation components of Catholic pacifism in our time has been represented—as we shall soon see—by the proponents (or shall we say the bearers) of that redemptive qualitative understanding of nonviolence as a spiritual discipline. Nonviolence is not a negation of an absence, but an affirmation. To reject violence is to affirm or (even more actively) to defend the integrity of that which one refuses to violate even in the name of some good cause. That active renunciation of violation and defense of the potentially violated is the active translation of the ancient virtue of "meekness," that quality of self-emptying which makes one an apt subject for inheriting the earth.

People who live this way tend to have disciples and houses in which they receive the needy and, therefore, to create the least ephemerally new forms of community. Yet the center of their concern is not a communitarian ethos. They tend to take symbolic stances of disobedience and to refuse to go along with the social patterns at certain points, but it would be a misunderstanding to think of them as, first of all, practitioners of civil disobedience. They feed the hungry or house the homeless or care for the sick, but, again, it would be a misinterpretation to begin with their effectiveness as innovators in the realm of institutionalized social services for especially disadvantaged groups of beneficiaries. All of these true, but derivative, descriptions are misunderstandings to the extent that they look away from the focus upon the cultivation of the image of Jesus the servant in the body and soul and spirit of the believer.

This forming of Christ is an end and not merely a means to some ethical goal. We can trust that in the measure in which that image is formed it will be productive of social goods and social values. Yet it is not because of those values that it is itself valuable, nor is its claim heightened by taking account of the probability of their being forthcoming. To be the kind of person who loves one's enemies, to be a servant, and to be meek are themselves more adequate definitions of doing the will of God than are tactical projections about how to maximize the likelihood of bringing about certain desirable states of the total social system.

This mode of ethical thought is not uniquely or narrowly Roman Catholic. It can also make sense for persons in other religious and social systems. Yet it is more at home in Catholicism than in mainstream Protestantism with its concern to avoid self-righteousness and its frequent preoccupation with social effectiveness. The importance of the movements to which we now turn is that they approach ethics in these other ways.

Approximately fifty years ago, on May 1, 1933, the circulation of a paper called *The Catholic Worker* began in the streets of New York City. It was the beginning of the public testimony of two highly independent and original laypersons. Dorothy Day, after a confused wandering through early adulthood as a social radical and religious agnostic, became a Roman Catholic by adult conversion in connection with the birth of her daughter.[4] Her background concern with the labor movement and her special skills as a journalist came into disciplined focus through the encounter with Peter Maurin, an autodidact French immigrant representing, in a simplified yet intellectually demanding way, the heritage of French Catholic personalism.[5]

---

[4] Dorothy Day (1897-1980) was born in Brooklyn, spent many of her growing-up years in Chicago, moved back to New York in 1924, and was received into the Catholic Church in 1927. She met Peter Maurin late in 1932.

[5] Peter Maurin (1877-1949) was born in France and entered the Christian Brothers at age sixteen. He emigrated to Canada in 1909 and quickly moved toward a nomadic life of working wherever he could find it. He eventually settled down in upstate New York, and he traveled to New York City as often as work allowed. He introduced himself to Dorothy Day in 1932.

The social base of the movement they founded was a network of "houses of hospitality": homes opened in many major
American cities ready to receive the hopeless poor at the bottom of society. These homes were created by volunteer workers
and supported by gifts from sympathetic Catholic parishes. This
solidarity in principle with the poor was unconditional; it was
not formally tied to Catholic parish or diocese structure, nor did
it make any religious claims upon the people who were fed and
housed. The workers in the hospitality house lived in voluntary
poverty and residential community, thus creating, in effect, a
kind of new religious congregation, although one with no interest
in seeking accreditation from the hierarchy as such. Each house
understood itself, in a sense, as a daughter to the center in New
York, but there was no defined policy concerning authority of
one house over others.

Secondly, the work of the Catholic Worker Movement was
its continuing publication *The Catholic Worker*. It was sold in the
streets for "a penny a copy" and to this day still does not have
regular subscription arrangements to cover its costs. It is an instrument of lay education communicating—in argumentative but non-
academic, popular yet sometimes spiritually profound ways—the
vision of wholesome human community which arose out of the
fusion of French personalism, the teachings of *Rerum Novarum*
(and soon *Quadragesimo Anno*), and the encounters with socialism
and sociology, illuminated as well by a reappropriation of simple
conversation with the Scriptures in liturgy and devotion.[6]

Although the primary focus of the movement until 1938 was
in the realm of social justice and God's concern for the poor in
the present and for a just society in the future (which led to a wide
expansion of *The Catholic Worker* so that 190,000 copies of the
journal were sold), Day and Maurin found it obvious and nearly
automatic that they should also be pacifists. At the cost of much

---

[6] *Rerum Novarum* (*The Condition of Labor*) is an encyclical written by Pope Leo
XIII and issued on May 15, 1891; *Quadragesimo Anno* (*After Forty Years*) is an
encyclical written by Pope Pius XI and issued on May 15, 1931. Both can be found
in David J. O'Brien and Thomas A. Shannon, eds., *Catholic Social Thought: The
Documentary Heritage* (Maryknoll, N.Y.: Orbis, 1992), 9–80.

support, they were the strongest voice within the Roman Catholic Church of North America against the simple acceptance of war as a moral response to the reopening hostilities in Europe. This pacifism did not arise, in any way, from a lack of realism about the evils of fascism, nor from optimism about the possibility of bringing about a better world soon by promoting international disarmament. They simply discerned in violence as such a denial of the newness of the life of faith as dramatically manifested in Jesus and the Sermon on the Mount but also as sustained through the centuries by monks and martyrs. Sometimes this meant detachment and nonparticipation in a militaristic society; other times, it meant witnessing action of a nonviolent kind. The rejection of war is not a casuistic refinement in the application of the criteria of the just war, but a holistic unfolding of the virtues of faith, hope, love, meekness, and the peacemaking and hunger for righteousness to which Jesus' beatitudes pointed.

Despite this moral radicality, Dorothy Day and the Catholic Worker Movement were profoundly traditional in their understanding of the Catholic life of piety and community. Traditional Marian devotions, fasting, retreats, belief in miracles, and devotion to the sacrament sustained a strong rootage in tradition and in the parishes. Despite nonconformist actions, there was no rebellion against episcopal authority. This obedience did not mean lack of critical perspective. Once, Catholic Worker demonstrators supported a labor union action of grave diggers against the cemeteries administered by the archdiocese of New York. Yet, through a number of priests who served the movement as chaplains, theological consultants, and agents of liaison to the chancery, the movement maintained its strong Catholic identity. It thereby made accessible to America the vision of the moral life of God's people which in other ages had been carried by religious orders when they saw themselves as agencies of spiritual renewal and pastoral care.

The Catholic Worker was the only moral support available for a handful of young Catholic men who took the position of conscientious objectors during World War II. The legislation providing for obligatory military service during World War II recognized the special status of conscientious objector for people "who by religious training and belief were opposed to all use of force." This applied to the so-called peace churches. It was not understood as a very important concession by the state, since the number of individuals from those churches would be very small. It was easier for the military authorities to grant the privilege of alternative service to young Quakers and Mennonites, rather than to deal with their conscientious disobedience in the training camps. The law, however, did not recognize Roman Catholics as conscientious objectors in principle, since the "religious training and belief" assumed to be operative in their communion provided that wars may be just. Nevertheless, a few courageous and persistent individuals were able to get local government agencies to recognize them as the moral equivalent of conscientious objectors. They were assigned, like Mennonites and Quakers, to manual service in forestry and hospitals, and occasionally reported on the way such service assignments deepened their convictions in *The Catholic Worker*.

In the early 1960s, a circle of Catholic Worker volunteers created another group and another magazine called *Pax Bulletin*. They arranged to be represented in Rome during the Second Vatican Council, in order to promote understanding, on the part of the bishops, of the nonviolent position and its increasing importance in the face of the armament race. They also created a "Catholic Peace Fellowship," affiliated with the International Fellowship of Reconciliation.[7] Their initial activity was primarily focused on opposition to the Vietnam War and on seeking modifications in the United States Selective Service laws which would allow for selective conscientious objection. From these circles, there arose, in 1968, a group of activists committing specific works of civil disobedience directed against the Vietnam

---

[7] The two groups to which Yoder refers grew out of the Catholic Worker Movement. The first group, formed in 1961–1962, was an American affiliate of the British Pax Association. It has now merged with the American affiliate of the Pax Christi Movement (the official international Catholic peace movement). The second group, formed in 1964, became the Catholic Peace Fellowship. It focuses on conscientious objection and regularly publishes *The Sign of Peace*.

War and especially against the conscription which obliged young men to participate in that war, even if they did not wish to. Three persons, in addition to those at the heart of *The Catholic Worker*, represent the depth and variety of this new movement.

Thomas Merton, a brilliant cosmopolitan educated in both France and the United States, was led to become a Trappist through his personal journey, and he used his very great skills as a journalist and publicist in the service of his new commitments.[8] His autobiographical description of his conversion and vocation, *The Seven Storey Mountain*, became immensely popular and contributed to the vocations of numerous young men in the following decades.[9] His early scholarship and publications as a monk were devoted very traditionally to the history of the contemplative life and to the disciplines which he was responsible to teach as novice master in the monastery at Gethsemani. In the late 1950s, however, he was drawn to a special degree of involvement (though he did not leave his monastery then) in the civil rights movement; similarly, in the next decade, he entered into the growing dissent about the Vietnam War. His writing increasingly turned to social criticism and to the history of nonviolence, including some of the accounts of the martyrs in the European war experience. He became one of Gandhi's prominent American interpreters. His prominence in the Catholic world contributed greatly to winning a hearing for the other, younger, Catholic pacifists.

James Douglass, a younger, lay theologian, was one of the "lobbyists" at Vatican II and was drawn to the mission of systematic literary expression.[10] His book *The Nonviolent Cross*, and his later *Resistance and Contemplation*, present a broad synthesis of Christian nonviolence, Gandhian tradition, Christian and non-Christian contemplative traditions, and the impact of the

---

[8] Thomas Merton (1915–1968) was born in France, moved to America to study at Columbia in 1935, was baptized in 1938, and was ordained in 1949.

[9] See Thomas Merton, *The Seven Storey Mountain* (New York: Harcourt, Brace, 1948).

[10] James Douglass founded the Ground Zero Center for Nonviolent Action in Poulsbo, Washington, and later founded a Catholic Worker house in Birmingham, Alabama.

European Holocaust.[11] Since the early 1970s, Douglass has been leading communities of resistance on the West Coast of the United States and Canada.

The reappropriation of the contemplative style of Eastern religion provides, for Douglass, a new form and a new élan for the unity of spirituality and nonviolence which the Catholic Worker Movement had represented in a more traditional framework of piety. The meaning of repentance as the constant inward dimension of the struggle for justice opens up the otherwise impossible way of nonviolent liberation, despite the hostility of our apocalyptic world. There are forms of resistance to evil which are not so fundamental as to represent this entire *metanoia*. Not all resistance has the vulnerability and readiness for the sacrifice of the cross. The cross is not a tactic of resistance; it is, first of all, God's means of reconciliation. The resistance to which the cross draws us is not an instrument of manipulating the powers who otherwise oppress us, except very secondarily; it is, first of all, a participation in the way of God with his rebellious cosmos.

Daniel Berrigan is a Jesuit whose first sensitivity to matters of social justice was developed through his presence in the parental home of the Catholic Worker of the 1930s.[12] His growing consciousness was nourished during a time in Europe when he met the Worker-Priest movement, and by a visit to South Africa where he first saw *apartheid* in its worst form. His brother, Philip, also a priest, was a missionary in the Josephite community, which worked especially amidst the American black population. Berrigan was thus led into the same stream of resistance as the persons already mentioned. To this he added his special gifts as poet and publicist and his special discipline as a Jesuit. He thus

---

[11] See James Douglass, *The Non-Violent Cross: A Theology of Revolution and Peace* (Eugene, Ore.: Wipf and Stock, 2006), and *Resistance and Contemplation: The Way of Liberation* (Eugene, Ore.: Wipf and Stock, 2006).

[12] Daniel Berrigan (b. 1921) was born in Minnesota, joined the Jesuits right out of high school in 1939, and was ordained in 1952. In 1980, he, his brother, and six others started the Ploughshares Movement, which committed intentional acts of vandalism targeted at nuclear installations. He continues to be a prolific writer and activist.

became the most visible participant in the various actions of civil disobedience directed, first, against the Vietnam War and, more recently, against atomic arms, serving several terms in prison as a result.

There is no way to quantify the weight of these few people or of the few hundreds who have been close to them in the last years. Their originality in facing contemporary reality more honestly than the rest of the church, and their profoundly traditional reappropriation of the vision of the Christian moral life rooted in contemplation and spirituality—rather than in the casuistry of justified violence—have contributed powerfully to a new awareness among American Catholics that being Christian may call for a fundamental critique of the conformity of the churches to the modern militarized world. In this way, they provided a background atmosphere for the other phenomena to which we shall turn in another lecture.[13]

We see emerging in the experience of these people a phenomenon which, in another lecture, I pointed out was of central importance in interpreting the meaning of Tolstoy or Gandhi or the other later witnesses.[14] These people are involved in a process of transformation. Some of them are "converts" in the formal sense of turning to a religion they formerly did not adhere to. Others of them are "converted" in the sense of the deep inward turning about in mind and spirit. Still others yield themselves to a never-ending process of *metanoia* as a renewing work of the Holy Spirit to make mankind peaceable through the transformation of character from the inside out and from the bottom up.

That the recovery of a peace vision comes to individuals by means of conversion also means, by implication, that the Christian peace community sees itself as a diaspora minority. Triumphalism is banished automatically, not through an intellectual self-critical operation of correcting for false consciousness, but through the renewal of a moral commitment which does not, at the outset, take account of whether it can impose its will on society through

---

[13] See chapter 10, pp. 121–32.
[14] See chapter 3, pp. 39-48.

legislation or penitential discipline. In this way, something of the posture of the early Christians has been rediscovered without any theory about the model of the free church, like those which have been developed in Protestantism. It is that restoration of original Christianity which we are seeing at work in our day, such as has not been the case with the same breadth or depth since the age of Francis. That is the privilege of living in our age.

Chapter 10

Varieties of Catholic Peace Theology II
Professors and Pastors

Thus far we have been observing developments in the unofficial Roman Catholic peace thought. Now we move to a more official level. The "professors" mentioned in our title are described by that term not so much because of formal employment in academic institutions, but rather because of the educative impact of their expository role. John Courtney Murray did serve as an instructor in theology in Jesuit theological faculties, yet the publications and research with which we are concerned was not a part of his primary academic responsibility.[1] Far beyond his teaching of Jesuit seminarians in the period between the world wars, he became the most authorized interpreter of Catholic social thought, especially when speaking with Protestants, especially in the realms of democracy and religious liberty.

John A. Ryan, while often occupied as a university teacher, was best known because of his continuing function in church agency administration. He was an advisor for matters of social concern to the National Catholic Welfare Conference and was responsible in that connection for bridging the distance between episcopal theology and lay Catholic social leadership.[2] Ryan is to

---

[1] John Courtney Murray (1904–1967), a Jesuit, was ordained in 1933, received a doctorate in sacred theology in 1937, and was the editor of *Theological Studies* from 1941 until his death.

[2] John A. Ryan (1868–1945) attended and eventually taught at The Catholic University of America.

be credited more than any other person for the fact that, by 1940, everyone understood that there was such a thing as a specific body of thought called "Catholic social teachings" that could be applied in a systematic way across the agenda of contemporary concerns. He was best known for, and perhaps most original in, his interpretation of the "living wage," which took direction from *Rerum Novarum* and which clashed with dominant American "market" doctrine, with liberal socialism, and in some ways with trade unionism. Had he been in Europe, he would have been chaplain to a Catholic student or labor movement or to a Christian democratic party.

In this role, Ryan drafted popular educational documents, like his social catechism, and textbooks, like *Catholic Principles of Politics*.[3] He was the founding and leading figure in the Catholic Association for International Peace, a volunteer educational agency active in both Great Britain and North America between the wars. The substance of Ryan's teaching about the morality of war was intentionally not original. What was original was the fact that he made an accessible and applicable set of guidelines for real political responsibility out of a vague and neglected tradition. Ryan interlocked bold legal customs, more-recent legal conventions, and ancient moral principles in a compendium that was intended to be practically usable. As such, he could not avoid raising the possibility of an obligation on the part of Christians in political-military responsibility to accept national sacrifices rather than to prosecute war unjustly. Yet that eventuality did not need to be looked at very seriously.

John Courtney Murray, S.J., was best known for his advocacy of religious liberty and a democratic, pluralistic vision of society. Frowned upon in previous decades, this position came into its own in Vatican II. However, Murray spoke with the same authority, though less frequently, on the issue of war. He insisted, as others did not, that to accept honestly the just war tradition means a readiness to accept defeat rather than prosecute a war unjustly.

---

[3] See John A. Ryan and Francis J. Boland, C.S.C., *Catholic Principles of Politics* (New York: Macmillan, 1940).

Murray was no defeatist. He did not believe that that tragic alternative would be unavoidable usually or always, but he insisted that the possibility needed to be reaffirmed if moral reasoning about war was to be responsible.

In 1959 Murray wrote, in the pamphlet *Morality and Modern War*, that both the stated goal of "unconditional surrender" and the resort to massive obliteration bombing of cities in the Second World War had been immoral.[4] Murray had begun that argument with an important reminder. Although the just war tradition has been "on the books" as the official doctrine of the churches, this does not mean that it had been effectively held to and applied. Whereas outside critics, whether pacifistic or humanistic, would look at the history of Western "Christian" nations as an example of the meaning of the doctrine of just war and would then be critical of the churches, or even of the Christian faith as such, for letting modern war happen, Murray insists that the doctrine had not been applied. Therefore, the just war doctrine should not be held to blame for what the majority of Western Christians had been doing for centuries, even though they claimed to be following it.

He wrote in 1959:

I think that the tendency to query the uses of the Catholic doctrine on war initially rises from the fact that it has for so long not been used, even by Catholics. That is, it has not been made the basis for a sound critique of public policies and as a means for the formation of a right public opinion . . . I think it is true to say that the traditional doctrine was irrelevant during World War II. This is no argument against the traditional doctrine. The Ten Commandments do not lose their imperative relevance by reason of the fact that they are violated. But there is place for an indictment of all of us who failed to make the tradition relevant.[5]

---

[4] See John Courtney Murray, *Morality and Modern War* (New York: Council on Religion and International Affairs, 1959).

[5] Murray, *Morality and Modern War*, 15.

What Ryan had said in a sketchy hypothesis before World War II, and what Murray said as an *a posteriori* condemnation after Hiroshima, two isolated individuals had said before.

John Kenneth Ryan (not the same John Ryan mentioned above), in a theology dissertation approved by The Catholic University of America in 1934 and published as a book in 1940, seems to have been the first scholar in Catholic moral theology to look seriously at what the looming prospect of air war against cities was going to mean morally.[6] He was followed in 1944 by a better-known Jesuit, John Ford, in an article in the Jesuit periodical *Theological Studies*.[7] Their argument was clear and was expertly formulated in classical just war terms. If the already existing technical potential for the aerial bombing of the cities was ever to be used, it would be immoral. No amount of manipulation of the traditional doctrines of double effect, and no possible redefinition of what constitutes combatant status in a modern society could possibly reach so far as to declare licit the bombing of cities.

And that was all there was in America. In Great Britain, there was a broad debate in the houses of Parliament and in the press, but the debate did not seriously involve Catholic churchmen or spill over to America.

The theme had been set out, but it never became widely noticed until after Hiroshima. A few small books were published in the late 1950s—several of which took in principle a position we have come to call "nuclear pacifism"—yet somehow none of them commanded public attention beyond limited academic circles, and none claimed the attention of bishops or synods.

The second symbol in our title, "pastor," points to a different way of thinking about ethics in which the primary consideration is not logical consistency but the quality of community. In a village or small parish, the rule of the pastor/priest, when there is controversy among the faithful, is neither to take sides as an

---

[6] See John Kenneth Ryan, *Modern War and Basic Ethics* (Milwaukee, Wis.: Bruce Publishing, 1940).

[7] John C. Ford, S. J., "The Morality of Obliteration Bombing," *Theological Studies* 5, no. 3 (1944): 261–309.

advocate nor to judge as if he were neutral or outside the conflict. He seeks rather to mediate by being present to both parties and by pleading with them to resolve their conflict without escalating anger and destruction.

In a similar way, it has been the function of the bishops of Rome for generations to represent such a goal of world reconciliation. Already, Benedict XV sought to transcend the polarity of World War I.[8] He did not seek, as a moralist or a jurist, to adjudicate the case and to determine whether the Catholics of France or the Catholics of Germany were fighting an unjust war and should cease hostility. This might have been called for by a consistent application of the just war tradition, but it was not attempted, although the bishops in both of the above countries published documents claiming the justice for their side. Instead, what Benedict did was to pray and to plead for peace, to remind both parties that hostility must one day end, that even in the midst of battle they must maintain policies and attitudes which would not make peace impossible later, and that they should be ready to accept some sacrifice.

As the village analogy illustrates, what is going on here is not normative moral teaching in the sense that henceforth every believer must do what the pope says, even though the just war tradition would seem to call for that, or at least enable it. Nor is what is going on a judicial process, deciding which party in a given war is fighting for a just cause or has been using improper means. The tradition would also seem to call for that. It is possible to evaluate this observation to the effect that the papal messages do not make much use of the just war tradition as itself constituting a part of the mosaic of negative evidence on the claim that that tradition is the tradition that genuinely informs Catholic moral identity. The just war tradition is *one* Catholic tradition, not *the* official one, and not always operative, as I have argued elsewhere.

One further stone in the negative mosaic is the observation that these papal "pastoral" messages never invite Christians to disobey unjust governments or unjust orders, that is, to take a

---

[8] Benedict XV (1854–1922) served as pope between 1914 and 1922.

position of selective conscientious objection, as the theory would demand. The appeal is rather to the need for an international authority to keep the peace, that is, for a new level where the vision could be renewed which calls for an agency to express moral judgments from above the parties to the conflict and to enforce those judgments with political and perhaps even military sanctions.

The posture of Pius XII in World War II was not very different. He renewed Benedict's pattern of addressing a Christmas message to the world pleading for peace. In one of these (Christmas 1944), he enunciated a new definition of the just war to the effect that a war of aggression could never be just.[9] Yet his attitude toward the Catholic citizens of the belligerent nations did not attempt to provide firm moral instruction. Rather, he continued to take the pose of the pastor to the world.

We are just now celebrating the twentieth anniversary of the next major step in papal pastoral responsibility, namely, the promulgation of *Pacem in Terris*.[10] Even in 1963, the papal text is not primarily moral instruction; it is admonition. There are a few passages which have provoked extensive exegetical debate by specialists in international law because of the particular way they speak of the decreased justification of war in view of modern weapons which are less capable of discrimination. *Pacem in Terris* does not lend itself to great clarity of explication. Yet as a response to the fright which the Cuban crisis of October 1962 gave all the peoples of the globe, the pope's proclamation raised seriously the level of awareness that new military technology represented a yet-undisciplined threat and also prepared the way for the Vatican Council to make comparable statements.

Yet while the world church was beginning to denounce the immorality of nuclear deterrence, the churches in the nations

---

[9] Pius XII (1876-1958) served as pope from 1939 to 1958. His actions during and after World War II are complex and continue to be debated. The particular text referred to here was called "Democracy and a Lasting Peace." See *Pius XII and Democracy: Christmas Message of Pope Pius XII, December 24, 1944* (Whitefish, Mont.: Kessinger Publishing, 2006).

[10] See David J. O'Brien and Thomas A. Shannon, eds., *Catholic Social Thought: The Documentary Heritage* (Maryknoll, N.Y.: Orbis, 1992), 129-62.

possessing nuclear armament were not bringing the message from Rome home to their national hierarchies. Was the reason for the lacuna an irrational patriotism? Was it intellectual laziness? Or was it perhaps the fruit of a deep conviction that the question was insoluble? At any rate, little progress was made within the thinking of Catholic citizens within any of the nuclear powers to apply the logical import of the moral statements already made by the popes and the council.

Only in this decade has that picture begun to change. It began again in a pastoral way, moved not by a professor's concern to be consistent but by a shepherd's desire to nurture. One bishop in America was approached by a layman of his diocese who had been working in the factory manufacturing nuclear warheads for missiles for years. He had come to the conviction that the weapons he was working on could not possibly be used in a just way. Therefore, he asked whether it was morally proper for him to continue to make his living producing them. The bishop was drawn into studying the matter because of the layman's conviction.

Another bishop had the base for the submarines bearing nuclear-tipped missiles in his diocese when the news was becoming widely known that the nuclear arsenal was being built up very rapidly. James Douglass (of whom I spoke in a previous lecture)[11] and a community of like-minded dissenters had been maintaining a visible presence near the base with occasional processions or actions of nonviolent direct action for some years. Bishop Raymond Hunthausen of Seattle was obliged to think more seriously about the possibility that these weapons, which constituted primary targets for a possible enemy first strike, would not only be dangerous to the people of his city and diocese, but also to think that, if used against any enemy, these weapons would bring about the destruction of innocents on an absolutely unjustifiable scale.[12] Thus, in the summer of 1980, he began speaking in public about his opposition to the nuclear arms race. He began thinking

[11] See chapter 9, pp. 107–20.
[12] Raymond Hunthausen (b. 1921) was ordained in 1946 and served as the archbishop of Seattle from 1975 to 1991.

in public about what possible means citizens might use to gain a hearing for their conscientious convictions. He asked whether the withholding of taxes would be an appropriate gesture. This hypothetical suggestion caught the attention of the public far more than he had intended or expected. After several more months of serious study, consultation, and prayer, Hunthausen did make and announce the decision that, beginning in April 1981, he would withhold a portion of his personal federal income tax as an expression of his refusal to share responsibility for the growing threat of nuclear destruction.

This exceptional intensity of visible individual commitment coincided with the growing degree of responsibility which national episcopal conferences have been encouraged to take since Vatican II. The regular meetings of the bishops of the United States have become increasingly important. This became the occasion for a study project of a greater weight and originality than had ever been undertaken previously. A drafting commission of five bishops, supported by research staff, calling upon experts of many kinds, gathering representatives from religious orders as well, prepared three drafts of a document in the course of the last thirteen months. The document, entitled "The Challenge of Peace: God's Promise and Our Response," was presented to the conference of bishops on May 2–3.[13] This text reaches a new level of both technical and theological discipline and originality. It properly concludes my present report.

The question constantly recurs when church authorities speak to nonecclesiastical matters: are they going beyond their authority? The document includes a defense of the appropriateness of the church's providing moral teaching to the faithful, as well as the paramount value of peace as the church's concern for human history. The political and technological dimensions of the problems have been studied at great depth, including interviews with numerous qualified experts from the most varied disciplines and

---

[13] The final text was later published, in 1983, as "The Challenge of Peace: God's Promise and Our Response." See O'Brien and Shannon, *Catholic Social Thought*, 492–571.

political orientations and including spokesmen for the past and present American governments. The bishops can in no way be accused of speaking of matters in which they are not competent: the study commission has become more informed than most of the journalists who accuse them of not being expert.

After having established the urgency of peacemaking and the seriousness of the nuclear threat, the report moves to a survey of the sources for moral judgment in the matter. At this point, the bishops refer to the position of Christian nonviolence and pacifism first. They name individual representatives of this conviction, including the late Dorothy Day and Martin Luther King Jr. They state that this position is worthy of a new hearing, especially since the call of Vatican II for "a whole new way of thinking" with regard to war. This is the first point at which the statement represents genuine innovation. For centuries, the just war tradition has so dominated official Catholic thought (on the part of professional theologians and churchmen) that it had been practically taken for granted that nonviolence must be wrong. Yet as a matter of record this was not true. The just war doctrine, although widely accepted, has never been promulgated by a council or pope, and the pacifist position has never been declared heretical. The pacifist position has always been represented in the Roman Catholic communion by individuals and religious communities and has been represented in Catholic piety by many of the saints. The American bishops' document thus restores a historic complementarity between the just war tradition and principled nonviolence as two ways to seed peace. This renewed recognition that one proper response to violence is simply to reject it morally is a landmark in modern Catholic thought.

Just as much a landmark is the shift in how the just war tradition itself is understood. In the formative epoch of Catholic political thought, the just war tradition had been conceived of as concrete and precise in the limitations it fixed for justifiable violence. It was assumed possible to determine the injustice of a particular war, or cause, or strategy, or weapon, and then effectively to proscribe its use and to subject to canonical discipline whoever would not respect that prohibition. Since early modern times,

however, that effective potential for restraint has largely evapo-
rated, as I indicated more fully in another lecture.[14] The growth
of the notion of absolute national sovereignty, the philosophical
impact of cynical political theories like that of Machiavelli, the
development of techniques of warfare decreasing the possibility
of discriminating use, and the growth of political ideologies tend-
ing to absolutize a cause as if it were far more than the selfish
interest of a particular nation all had a share in weakening any
potential for effective restraint which the theory might originally
and logically have exercised. The American bishops are, therefore,
reclaiming long-lost territory when they propose to make effective
use of just war reasoning as an instrument for effective restraint.
They briefly report the history of the doctrine, its several criteria,
and their application. Then the concentration upon the criterion
of noncombatant immunity leads directly to challenging the possibility of ever using nuclear weapons justly.

This concrete innovation then leads to another: the bishops
are willing to face the possibility that this moral position might
set them against the official armament policies of the present
government of their country. This reopens the possibility of resistance as a possible Christian response to a government making
unjust demands. The Catholics of the United States have seldom
been ready to take "unpatriotic" positions. For generations, as
recent immigrants, they needed to try very hard to prove to other
Americans that they were American. Only recently has the liberal-
ization of abortion law led them to a more critical stance toward
government as a whole. Yet that had not been connected with the
matters of war or the sacredness of life in other areas. Now bishops
are leading the way in thinking about what the limits to morally
proper service to one's government (or participation otherwise in
community life) might be and if it should be the case that the support which a government is asking for is morally improper.

These comments have drawn much attention to the document from outside the Roman Catholic communion. Numerous
interpreters of political matters in the academic and journalistic

---

[14] See chapter 4, pp. 49–61.

professions have considered it their duty to instruct the bishops, first of all, that it is improper for religious figures to speak to political matters and, secondly, that it would have been proper if they had spoken of political matters less critically. The fact remains that, at the very beginning, the notion of the just war had been intended to provide a possibility for independent moral judgment concerning the plans of governments and their claims upon their subjects. This fact had been so largely lost from view that this reproach seemed natural to them. The fact that, in pre-Renaissance times, bishops had actually intervened more actively in political conflicts—sometimes to mediate and sometimes to menace with excommunication the parties guilty of not respecting the inherited moral tradition—was completely lost from view. These journalists and Catholic lay people in political responsibility felt that the just war notion simply means that political decision makers may use violence whenever they feel it to be authentically in the national interest. It is at this point that the new authority and responsibility of the bishops as pastors has rediscovered a dimension of moral depth that had been radically lost—and was profoundly needed—ever since the breaking up of the vision of medieval unity under the impact of the Renaissance, Reformation, and Enlightenment.

Once these assumptions were stated, the implications for public policy had to follow. The bishops declared

a. that no use of nuclear weapons, whether as first strike or in retaliation, can be morally acceptable;
b. that the notion of a "limited nuclear war" is unrealistic;
c. that the concept of "deterrence" (i.e., of retaining nuclear weapons and threatening their use in order to avoid their use), if acceptable at all, must be only provisional and linked with moves toward disarmament and the avoidance of weapons calculated for counterpopulation or first-strike use;
d. that Christians in every social setting must make conscientious decisions concerning their personal moral responsibilities;
e. that important steps must be taken toward reducing the danger of war, including the development of nonviolent means

of conflict resolution and the strengthening of the institutions of world order.

These conclusions are, in themselves, not startling; others had been advocating them for decades. What must be recorded as a landmark is the readiness of an entire national episcopal collegium to state them together, in a strong majority, and in the face of widespread warnings of government disapproval. It is in this respect that American Catholicism has entered a new phase of civil courage and pastoral responsibility.

Chapter 11

Varieties of Catholic Peace Theology III
Latin American Models

Clearly the most widely watched new development in Catholic theology in the Western hemisphere in the last decade has been the movement called "liberation theology." There are theologies of liberation being elaborated in religious traditions other than the Roman Catholic and in favor of oppressed populations other than the poor in Latin America. Those other themes and those constituencies would be equally worthy of study. I do not suggest that they are all derived from the Latin American Catholic thinkers of whom I speak. Nonetheless, the numbers, quality, and visibility of the work from this milieu merit special attention just now.

I need to begin with descriptive reporting, yet I trust that much of what I report will not be new to my listeners. A brief descriptive introduction may both enlarge and narrow the frame of reference for our attention to the issues of war and peace.

The theme is enlarged by locating it within a development in Western theology which reaches back to the beginning of the century. In the early decades of our century, the label "social gospel" was given to a movement seeking anew to integrate the concerns of the gospel with social justice. In the age of initial decolonization, something similar developed in the so-called "third world" under the rubric of a "theology of revolution," which circulated especially within ecumenical and missionary Protestantism. Until 1970, the concern of these movements was to restore a more organic or holistic vision of the purpose of God for humanity by

rejecting the various kinds of dichotomies which have traditionally reserved religious concern for the realm of ritual or of inward
spirituality without direct attention to the pertinence of faith for
the social order. Much of what had to be struggled for through
those decades seems to us to be somewhat ordinary now. Yet in
every generation there is a new population for whom the issue
needs to be worked through again.

Thus, the ideas promoted by the theologians of liberation
are not new. Some of them are explicitly derived from European
theologians, whether in the fields of biblical exegesis or ecclesiology. Other components are derived from the experience of the
North Atlantic nations without being critically aware of that
borrowing. What is new is the projection of that vision of social
justice as part of the gospel in that part of the globe where the
institutional power of the Roman Catholic Church has, for centuries, been great and unchallenged and where that power had,
until recently, been allied with the status quo. The special challenge of those forms of economic and political oppression under
which most of Latin America suffers correlates with the heritage
of intellectual and institutional domination of the continent by
Catholicism. This context provides exceptional resonance to the
new theologians who work through what it means to consider
oppression as a synonym for perdition, and liberation as a synonym for salvation.

What this change means for the internal structure of theology
can be reviewed very briefly:

a. It means reading the Bible as the narrative of God's liberating interventions, of which the exodus from Egypt is
   prototypical.

b. It means that the vocation of theology must be exercised not
   in abstract speculation but in the dialectic of liberating praxis
   and critical reflection.

c. It means that, in the practical dimensions of participating
   in the liberation as a human movement, use will be made
   of secular scientific insights, such as those tools of economic
   and historical analysis offered by Marxism.

d. It means that the church herself will be called to participate in movements of democratization and empowerment if she is to be a bearer of such a message to the nations.

From this introduction we need to move in two directions. The affirmative interaction between the themes these lectures have been dealing with and the development of theologies of liberation is one of mutual reinforcement between discussion of liberation as a general slogan and the rejection of war as a concrete social witness. The oppression under which the poor of the world suffer is, to a large extent, the price of the military mobilization imposed upon the world by the superpowers. This is the case, most simply, because the minerals, energy, and engineering intelligence invested in arms production are stolen from the commonweal, and most of these irreplaceable resources will never be used to feed or to educate or to transport the poor of the rest of the world. It is more directly the case because the superpowers, in their effort to deny to one another the control of the rest of the world, support the militarization of all of the nations they are able to bring under their dependency, nations which can ill afford to pay the price of militarization. To some extent, the superpowers give them tanks and planes as if it were economic aid; worse than that, however, they support internal distortions of the economy which also waste domestic resources on arms, on the maintenance of a standing army, and on the maintenance of social control by a military elite. The reason there is no great likelihood of effective social change toward greater justice in most of Latin America (since we are speaking now only of that continent) is that the North American military establishment considers any movement in that realm to be counter to its interests and considers it morally and politically justified that this hegemony be exercised over the hemisphere. It may be that elements of this self-righteousness on the part of the North American authorities are encouraged by some of the simple language with which "liberation" is occasionally equated with violent national uprisings.

In this way, we have ascended to the second level of dialogue with the theology of liberation. This level of dialogue can be initiated by returning to the very beginning of the story: that is, to the interpretation of the exodus.

A short-circuited image of Western history has led to an insufficiently critical analysis of what authentic freedom means. I point here not to a difference between law and gospel nor between secular and religious visions, but between complete and incomplete understandings of oppression and freedom.

A superficial understanding of modern history suggests that the most important happenings to further and safeguard human dignity have been revolutions. The British uprising in the age of Cromwell, the American Revolution of 1776, and the French Revolution of 1789 were followed by a wave of independence movements across South America through the nineteenth century. These were later joined by Russia, then China, etc., in our century. Since the history books have been written by the teachers placed in office by the victorious revolutionaries, it has been taught—and has come to be assumed—that each of these events was a major leap forward for human dignity, that the values they achieved could only have been achieved that way, and that the fundamental liberating impact of all of them has been of the same quality.

On the level of honest historical description, it is not the case that revolution generally liberates. Many of the "liberators" of nineteenth-century Latin America were feudal warlords or itinerant mercenary colonels fostering rebellion against the administration of Lisbon or Madrid in the interest of the autonomy of the local landed aristocracy. Thus, the Latin American experience itself refutes the notion that a national uprising generally produces a just society, even though the legend of "freedom through revolution" has continued to be the dominant myth of the Western world in both its liberal bourgeois and its Marxist variations.

What we are concerned about here is the inappropriateness of telescoping this myth into the biblical story of the exodus, which is of more fundamental importance than the fact that the myth of freedom through revolution is ambivalent in its own right. It is certainly true that the event of exodus is both historically and literarily the foundation of Hebrew identity. Who God is and who his people are, the reasons for their common life, and the nature of their common life are all derived from that foundational liberation. Yet its meaning is broader and deeper than what it comes to be associated with when equated with modern Western national rebellions.

The exodus event was not the origin of Hebrew identity but rather its renewal. That identity was already present in the midst of enslavement. Moses was instructed to introduce himself to the suffering descendents of Abraham as "the god of the fathers." If there had not been national unity in subjection, there would have been none to rise up and seize freedom. In a similar sense, liberation in our age does not begin with the enfranchisement of a formerly nonexistent body of people but presupposes a community whose identity and structures were alive under the yoke of slavery. This was true for the peoples whom Gandhi and King led toward greater liberty. Thus, rebellion is not the first stage of liberation but must be preceded by the development of community and consciousness. Political enfranchisement is not a prerequisite but a product of authentic community identity. The Latin American churches today demonstrate this knowledge by their focus on "consciousness" as the goal of education.

Nor was the exodus event a takeover. The Israelites did not seize power in Egypt; they went away and created a new polity around a new loyalty without an immediate territorial basis. If they had risen up and seized power in the cities of the Nile Valley instead of the exodus, they would have been one more in a long line of such invaders and usurpers to be swallowed up by Egyptian culture. Instead of that, they created a new pattern—as Abraham had begun to do before them and as Jeremiah and Jesus were to do later—not defined either by territory or by sovereignty but by the identity of the Lord around whom they gathered and to whom they pledged obedience.

The exodus event was not the end but only the beginning of the tribulations of Israel. They continued to fall into idolatry. They continued to doubt and disobey the God who had freed them and the human leaders whom God had used. Having been freed from the yoke of Pharaoh was an ambivalent blessing; some of them wished they could return. Most of them were guilty of unbelief in the purpose or power of the Lord to lead them. If anyone had thought that the exodus would inaugurate an age of justice (as many of our contemporaries have been encouraged to think that "the revolution" will do), that was soon refuted.

Not only was it refuted in the early years of wanderings in the desert, it was also refuted by centuries of trying to be a state like other nation-states in Palestine. God ultimately abandoned kingship as an inappropriate way for his people to live under his lordship. The preoccupation of theologies of liberation with the first half of the Old Testament thereby fails to learn the importance of the experience of exile for understanding God as liberator (which I have already referred to in another lecture).[1] What it means to be an Israelite or an Israeli may be spoken of as defined by the experience of kingship in Judea and Ephraim, but what it means to be Jewish was defined in the experience of diaspora since Jeremiah. The deepest and most powerful prophetic visions of the glory of God working itself out in a human history of peace and well-being are not visions of a new Davidic empire ruling from the Nile to the Euphrates with a rod of iron. Rather, it is the vision of a restored people and a restored Jerusalem—without an army and sometimes even without a temple, in some visions—to which the nations voluntarily come to learn the law of the Lord in order to live at peace without studying the arts of war and without fear of one another.

The other face of liberation—once bitter experience has told us that exodus alone does not bring fulfilled righteousness—is the acceptance of exile. YHWH, first of all, freed his people from the empire of Pharaoh by giving them the political form of a kind of civil government under Moses. But then he freed them again from the temptation to find their community's dignity in the power of an army or the glory of a royal house by creating the new possibility of life in the diaspora, *not as a punishment, but as mission*; not as temporary banishment, but as a way to keep on

---

[1] See chapter 6, pp. 73–84.

living and witnessing to the power of the one true God until the Messiah comes.

This dimension of the prophetic witness is also becoming a part of the conversation in Latin America now. It is no surprise that Protestant theologians, more accustomed to living as a minority, have more rapidly and wholeheartedly grasped this diaspora perspective within the theology of liberation. Rubem Alves, a Presbyterian of Brazil,[2] and Miguel Brun, a Methodist from Uruguay,[3] have been the theologians who first pointed most articulately in this direction. The memory of the message of Jeremiah should protect against an overly naive identification of the liberation promises by YHWH of Hosts with the next uprising promised by some particular local group of combatants. Not every group calling itself a liberation front is able either politically or ideologically to bring freedom. For the theologians of liberation to give their blessing too simply to the first pretender to the title of liberator is to exacerbate the risk of triumphalism if the next rebellion is successful, and of deep demoralization if it fails (as is more likely).

This points us to the originality of two contemporary Latin American Catholic liberation thinkers whose positions are less known and less systematic but, perhaps for that reason, are more promising as well.[4] They both represent a new vision which builds not only upon what we have said about Jeremiah but also on what an earlier lecture reported about James Douglass.[5] The experience of Gandhi and King, taken in a very broad sense as synthesized by Douglass, gives a new lease on life to the Catholic

---

[2] Rubem Alves (b. 1933) is probably best known for his A Theology of Human Hope (New York: Corpus Books, 1969).

[3] According to Yoder, Miguel Angel Brun wrote Concepto Cristiano de la Salvaciòn Hoy in 1970 but had been thinking about these for a while, as evidenced in his contributions to El Rincon Teolóico, the small publication of the Evangelical Mennonite Theological Seminary in Montevideo, Uruguay. See John H. Yoder, "The Wider Setting of 'Liberation Theology,'" The Review of Politics 52, no. 2 (1990): 295–96.

[4] The two thinkers Yoder introduces here, and will name later, are Dom Hélder Câmara and Adolfo Pérez Esquivel.

[5] See chapter 9, pp. 107–20.

vision for Christianizing general human moral values. We learn that it was wrong to Christianize the powers of imperialism, but we can baptize the tactics of Gandhi and King into Catholic social responsibility. Especially in the Latin American situation, where one can somehow count on the continuing Catholic loyalty of the common people and a widespread acceptance of a Catholic Christian worldview, this new instrument can constitute a new kind of natural commonsense way to Christianize the social order when the old ways of linking the church with state power failed or even betrayed their cause. This enables Catholics coming to this set of concerns for the first time to avoid stopping at the barriers set up by Anglo-Saxon Protestant "realism" with regard to the limited power of the democratic process and the difficulty of creating new social institutions, and also the barrier of Protestant conceptual consistency about deciding between nonviolence as a strategy of power and nonresistance as a gospel ethic. The misery of the masses of Latin America, the fact that there never has been genuine democracy, and the fact that most other kinds of governmental change have come through demonstrations in the streets increase the relative trust that one has in popular nonviolent movements in proportion to the loss of confidence in alternative processes of a more traditional kind, whether revolutionary or within the system. This approach is "catholic" in the sense that it is planted within a Catholic population and in that it shows no embarrassment about incorporating insights about both theory and tactics which have been learned from other places—even from India—within Catholic morality.

Douglass is listed here because of the specific way he seeks to learn from Gandhi and the specific way he expects love to be effective in a way that is especially appropriate to Latin America. We should, however, not forget the other elements in Douglass' synthesis:

a. Contemplation: that is, the cultivation of an alternative sense of what is real
b. Symbolic rather than efficacious considerations in nonviolent direct action

c. Cultivation of counterculture urban communal life styles: that is, his "resistance community" is a concept different from that of Dorothy Day and more like the later Berrigan.

Dom Hélder Câmara,[6] whose archdiocese is in the poorest region of Brazil (the Northeast), has been a leader in the councils of Brazilian bishops for decades. He has moved with increasing clarity to outspoken social criticism, to profound pastoral identification, and, at the same time, to contemplative and sacramental piety. He has, like many bishops, fostered the formation of "base communities": that is, local fellowships for moral and spiritual solidarity not dependent upon the specialized sacerdotal leadership. Under open attack from the nation's military government, he has been leading his people in the discovery of patterns of witness and empowerment which are not frustrated by the lack of immediate political prospect, as traditional liberation rhetoric would lead people to be. In a country where neither constitutional democracy nor violent revolution has any chance of bringing rapid social amelioration, the creativity of the diaspora community is the only way out.

Câmara grants that on the legal and theoretical levels the moral case for a violent revolution is strong. The overt and structural violence of the present regime demands the loyalty of its subjects and justifies those who would seek to change it. Those who believe that such change can come through clandestine militancy or guerrilla violence cannot be denied a certain heroic nobility. They are, however, factually wrong in their reading of the prospects for change. That their vision is spiritually less profound than the way of the cross is not a shortcoming that Câmara, as a patient pastor, would reprimand, although it is clear in his own writings that his perception of authentic liberating ministry is on that deeper level of the cross of the Messiah rather than the sword of the Zealot. He is a patient pastor; he honors the heroic nobility of the Zealot who sees nothing else to do.

[6] Dom Hélder Câmara (1909-1999) was the Catholic archbishop of Olinda and Recife (Brazil). Câmara received the Pacem in Terris Award (1975) for his work on behalf of the Brazilian poor.

It was a surprise to everyone, but most of all to the military rulers of Argentina, when the 1980 Nobel Peace Prize was awarded to Adolfo Pérez Esquivel. A painter and sculptor by profession, Pérez Esquivel was called into leadership of the International Peace and Justice Service in 1974. He had, on his own, created a journal, *Peace and Justice*, in 1973, which then became the organ of the newly created international network.[7] After traveling around Latin America, he was imprisoned in Argentina from April 1977 to June 1978. While he was in prison, a meeting of bishops from around the continent, which he had planned, was carried out in Bogota, Colombia, in November and December 1977. The meeting concluded with the adoption of a "charter of nonviolence in Latin America," projecting "evangelical nonviolence as a force for liberation."[8]

From that text, let me cite:

Nonviolence is lived in concrete action. As action, it has a relationship to the social reality, and thereby to all the power of institutionalized violence within that reality. It neither ignores nor camouflages that violence. Least of all does it admit its legitimation as necessary and inevitable. On the contrary, it forthrightly denounces violence as an optional product of the human mind and heart, and fruit of human beings' free decisions, choices, and preferences. Nonviolence is not to be confused with passivity, inertia, or the toleration of injustice.

Like all human activity, in order to be efficacious nonviolence must be persevering, clear in its objectives, and methodical in its procedure. Far from rejecting the mediation of social analysis, it considers such an analysis indispensable for discerning the real problems—of identifying concrete injustices along

---

[7] Adolfo Pérez Esquivel (b. 1931) continues to be active in promoting peace, human rights, and liberation. The organization to which Yoder refers here is known as the Servicio de Paz y Justicia (SERPAJ), and the journal is *Paz y Justicia*.

[8] Yoder is referring to the "Declaration of the International Meeting of Latin American Bishops on 'Nonviolence: A Power for Liberation,' November 28–December 3, 1977."

with their causes and deep mutual bonds. Nonviolent action intends to provoke changes in history. Its view of the human being and society stimulate it to use methods and acts of non-cooperation against unjust economic, political, and technological systems. As these acts of collective moral pressure mount up and accumulate, they begin gradually and systematically to withdraw all these unjust systems' support. And, they compel the discovery and construction—from its foundations to its pinnacle—of an alternative, socialized society.

Nonviolent action implants, by anticipation within the very process of change itself, the values to which the change will ultimately lead. Hence it does not sow peace by means of war. It does not attempt to build up by tearing down; neither does it contradict its own aspirations for a community of brothers and sisters by the very acts through which it seeks to transform society.

Nonviolent action perseveres. It is nourished by the conviction that the human person is of absolute worth. Our Christian faith gives to this conviction a powerful impetus. For we believe in the person and work of Jesus, the nonviolent One par excellence. . . .[9]

To be sure, the spirit of nonviolence is not a Christian monopoly. Still we do find in our faith and in the words and actions of the Lord Jesus a profound motivation and clear examples of nonviolent action in real life. In Christianity, then, such action is the incarnation of a way of living the gospel by coming to grips with the injustices of this world.

Hence, nonviolence must begin with the radical transformation of our personal lives. We must do violence to ourselves—

---

[9] See the English translation of the "Declaration" appended in Adolfo Pérez Esquivel, *Christ in a Poncho: Witnesses to the Nonviolent Struggles in Latin America*, trans. Robert R. Barr (Maryknoll, N.Y.: Orbis, 1983), 127.

we need to transcend the selfish instincts that divide us among ourselves and cut us off from our sisters and brothers. We have to conquer the temptation to accommodation and passivity by overcoming the fear that grips our hearts. We must uproot all the seeds of hatred, resentment, and vengeance that may have sprouted within us and that express themselves in our immediate interpersonal relationships. Nonviolence is a response to violence and oppression; only it is not a response in kind. It is not the product of an instinctual mechanism that will determinedly mete out measure for measure. It is a response welling up out of the deepest reaches of our interior liberty, giving us the capacity to repair human relationships by restoring a respect for personhood and freedom. The spirit of reconciliation never springs from cowardice or weakness. Christian forgiveness is the fruit of love and an act of freedom. It creates freedom in others.

We find the clearest example of the spirit of nonviolence in dialogue. We know how difficult it is to have a dialogue while it is easy to have two simultaneous monologues. In a monologue we seek to justify ourselves alone and to denounce the errors of the adversary alone. In a dialogue, on the other hand, we begin by seeking the truth that lies with the other side, the good there is in our adversary. We have to be honest enough to tell him or her what we have found. Next, dialogue requires us to raise our consciousness of the manner in which we ourselves in our lives have betrayed the truth we find in our adversary. Only then may we declare our own truth—in full knowledge that we have often been unfaithful to it, too, by our actions.

Finally—having completed the first three steps—we may proceed to the fourth. Now we may declare to our adversary the wrong we find in him or her, the injustice he or she is committing. But the manner of our declaration must be such as to engage our adversary to join us in a companionable journey up the road to justice, as we confess that all of us are sinners. Thus in a dialogue that is sincere, the liberating word is pronounced—

the word that delivers not only us but also our adversary as well from the oppression of the evil within us all.

To set out on the road of nonviolence means making a distinction between the wrong committed by the oppressor and his or her personhood. One must love the person and hate the evil. This is why nonviolent action may never have recourse to force or power. Indeed, it may never offend the oppressor by so much as an insulting word. On the contrary, in imitation of Christ, nonviolent persons will endeavor to live the spirituality of the Suffering Servant of Isaiah 53. They will avoid all spirit of domination over other human beings. They will eschew all signs of discrimination or superiority. They will seek serenity by means of an ongoing program of training in order to overcome their fear. They will live in truth, they will tell the truth, and they will defend the truth—but always with love.

Commitment to the spirit and mystique of nonviolence means taking up the challenge of following Jesus, all the way to his seeming human failure. For that failure became the seed of humanity's radical transformation. It is love, not violence or hatred, that will have the last word in history. Jesus' resurrection delivers us from the seeming absurdity of a meaningless death when we are crushed by the mighty ones of this world. His resurrection is the proclamation of a community of sisters and brothers among all men and women. For we are all children of the same Father who is in heaven.[10]

"It is love, not violence or hatred, that will have the last word in history." If that is the last word, say Câmara and Pérez Esquivel, it must be our word now.

---

[10] Pérez Esquivel, *Christ in a Poncho*, 126–27.

Index